SECRET MODERN
MONEY MECHANICS

Carlos Calçada Bastos

Index

Foreword

I believe in gratitude, I do believe in it and my first thanks are towards life that has been fascinating my existence daily for 57 years!

I wonder the reason why people lose the enthusiasm we all experienced in our earliest years. Every day is a NEW day, if only we could show up as "new", eager to live new experiences, exactly in the way we used to do when we were children!

Thanks to Tea Pecunia who works in publishing and pushed me into writing about the things I had been reading up for a long time and lazily stored up.

A deep thank you to my wife Maria who comes along with me in every step and adventure of my life and peacefully lets me apply to the research and the writing of this book.

To my parents that made of me a fertile ground in which I planted and still now I plant so many things.

Thanks to all my children that sustain me in all my evolutions and interests. Finally, a special thanks to my son Andrea Nuno that patiently looked after the layout, the cover and the fluency of information.

This book has been translated amateurishly from Italian, as such, the sentence structure doesn't always follow the standard English. We aim to have this book translated professionally in the future.

You only find it when you look for it

Before telling you what a small portion of the population knows about money, I am going to tell you how I got this knowledge.

I have no strong background that helps me do what I do. At 19 years old I worked as a waiter, but I have never thought to be just that. This could already help to start to think...

Never identify yourself with the job you do, whatever it could be, however noble it may seem!

Each one of us is much more than the job he chose. But if we choose to stand by this identification we will be trapped in that small area that defines it, precluding the possibility to explore other opportunities.

If today I live off of private income I have to thank this thought that went along with (me) my entire life, enabling me to reach leadership at 27 years old in a multinational company. Not much later, at the age of 35 I achieved maximum leadership.

Reached that goal, I decided to be a freelance and, after only 3 years, I decided to abandon this area of work to dedicate fully on something else.

For a long time I had been living off private income and once again... I find myself working in a totally different area.

Be aware that life has plenty of opportunities to offer everything we want, to anyone who is able to catch them!

Life makes no distinctions, as well as it poses no resistance, it simply moves in "its" flow, regardless of what we say or think.

It depends only on us if we put up resistance to its dynamics and live this tension.

As an ex-waiter I quickly learnt this principle. Thanks to it, I found out that our life has no complexity; once again "we" are in difficulty.

Obstacles do not exist!

Or rather, anything that we do not have familiarity with is "difficult", but only as long as we refuse to evolve on that specific subject!

Try and remember something that you could not do. An example I often use is learning a foreign language.

Go back with memory, to the first time you ever opened that book...damn! Each letter put together made a word that had no meaning, in addition to being unpronounceable.

Do you remember?

However, step by step, word after word, mistake after mistake...today that foreign language is no longer an obstacle.

The same reasoning applies with computers or any other thing. Don't you find it fascinating?

I do!

Every time that I encounter any difficulty on a specific topic, I instantly know life is whispering that I need to carry out homework on that specific topic, otherwise I will not go forward.

Do you understand why I affirm that difficulties do not exist?

Any difficulty vanishes by virtue of our skill and we acquire all our skills with practice.

The excuses we come up with to not train on a specific topic are not important... Life does not speak our language, therefore it does not understand our reasons, and it ends up proposing again the same difficulty.

This is why I firmly sustain that we go against life. Moreover, this is the reason I am fascinated watching the nonchalance which many people show facing life, despite their difficulties.

For 20 years I have been targeting towards Personal development and personal growth as my goal and it is more than 15 years that I help people to face life in an easy and pragmatic way, but maybe it has already been slightly grasped.

This is why, approximately 4 years ago, when I was 52 years old, I decided to explore the finance and economics world to escape from the usual routine of working in return of money.

I began applying all the dynamics I learned during the years I spent studying the aspects of life to introduce myself, firstly from a cultural point of view, into this model completely new to me.

As time passed by, the more I was coming in touch with people working in that field, the more I perceived that there is a universe kept far away from public attention. Keeping things from people is particularly easy in the modern days since their only desire is to distract themselves thanks to computers, television, social networks, text messaging, newspapers, internet...

Anything rather than being with ourselves!

We do not have to be surprised if asking someone "how are you?", the answer we receive is: "I'm taking it one day at a time".

Nothing more precise!!!

With these pages I want to share with you, in a simply way as my existence itself shows, some concepts and history of money and wealth, with the only purpose to make some information available that - used in the proper way- can change the life of a person.

I think that these things, as others more, should be taught in schools, but I am aware that education in schools is kept under control to keep a unanimous and unvarying community: a square society. A society that cannot, therefore, give a hard time.

Ultimately it is not economy or what else that is ruining our society, it is just a matter of "conformism", as a conventional attitude!

We think of ourselves as "special", but in the end we all dread to be considered different and so we keep "in line" with the social context (social mores).

We go on talking about diseases that affect our community, such as avian flu or cow madness just till the moment "someone" decides to go no longer the society let's us.

Let's look back at the homicide of Sarah Scazzi. For over a year, the media have been keeping the attention of the people on various tv shows dedicated to this case.

Did you know that an Ansa data of 26/04/2010 reveals that Italy is ranked first for "family homicides" in all Europe, with an average of one killing every two days? Approximately 180 each year!

Have you been you aware of this?

If the data is correct, why for over a year the media have been focusing only on this case? What about The remaining 179?!

As well as the case involving Captain Schettino and the Costa Concordia which sank.

Nowadays we know what type of flu will be coming, its name, the symptoms and the period when the vaccine will be available!

Couldn't you believe it?

Believe me, the real threat to our society is conformism.

Too little people choose to make some effort by evolving and expressing their own individuality, regardless of public opinion.

However, this gives birth to a whole new scenario so let's go get back to money and wealth.

Ability with money

Money - as life - does not consider obstacles or challenges that, as already stated before, pertain/concern exclusively to everyone as individual!

Whichever difficulty, faced with determination and resolution, disappears with the growth of our ability.

The same thing happens with money!!!

The real issue is not the difficulties we encounter, but our resistance to face them and take over.

Any skill or ability is defined by practice.

The question is:

"What are we specifically doing to acquire such ability?"

The crux of the question lies in the single word *"specifically"*.

The same reasoning applies to money!

What are we <u>specifically</u> doing to acquire a level of mastery with money and all its dynamics?

How much is costing us in stress, health, lifestyle, not to mention the loss of income, being ignorant in the matter?

Did you know that within the best workplaces of the future, an estimate of 60% lies in Ecology/Habitat/Welfare; but 25% is kept for Financial Advisors?

For how long do we want to stay hidden behind what financial advisors say?

Personally, I have nothing against financial advisors, many of them work at their best, but have to follow the strict guidelines of their employer, whether it is a bank or a holding company.

I wonder how could a financial "expert", after several years, be still in need to work for an employer, and ask for "permission" if he has to go to go to the dentist?

I wonder how couldn't he take advantage of his abilities. Could he? !

Anyway, the above sentences just want to be a provoc...Action, giving you homework, since the words will not change anything, but only the use you are going to do will make the difference.

Let's always keep in mind that life does not answer to wishes or necessities, it only answers to Actions.

Ability is not achieved by only going through the theoretical way.

Theory itself does not help to learn a foreign language... Neither it helps to cook... Ride a horse... Being a parent... Play cards... Play any musical instrument...

Mastery is acquired with Practice, with Actions! Therefore, using properly information make the difference of living, not the information itself.

Our "emotion" is our prophecy

In the competitive world it is said: "If you think you will lose, you've already lost."

The same principle applies to money: our mindset, therefore our approach to money, isn't just important, it is crucial.

Unfortunately, the society we live in/our social context, instill many negative construct on the money and this prevents us from entirely opening to it.

The most common stereotypes are:

"Money isn't everything"

True!

However In our society money is used for everything, starting from the mere survival: food, water, home, clothes.. It is used for healthcare, to give education to our children and ourselves, up to to charity work.

"Money makes us slaves"

False!

If anything, it's the other way round: It is the shortage of money that makes a human being addicted; this is the new slavery.

"Money does not buy happiness"

True!

Happiness is a "philosophy" that has nothing to do with the material world, but this does not mean that poverty brings us happiness.

"Money is vile" (?!)

How can an object be vile? It is like saying that the vile gun killed the victim. (?!)

Money is just what an individual uses it for.

And so on many many other prejudices. The truth is that money only offers "much more choice", that's all.

It gives the individual a wider pool of options in case of health emergencies, educational paths, charity work.

In other words, money is the means to take advantage of more opportunities.

Moreover, money highlights the individual's essence since it brings to surface the real nature of his behavior. In fact a vile person becomes even more vile because of the money he possesses. Likewise, if you think of an arrogant, benevolent or rude person.

Our perception of "speculators" is a trap, too.

A speculator is nothing more than a person that benefits from "favourable" circumstances, that is to say critical.

Do not forget that we all are speculators when we do compulsive shopping in a place that is closing for failure.

Moreover, during periods of crisis and recession, the speculators are those that put money into circulation, even if for their own benefit. But what would happen if they did not do that?!

Who else would help economic growth? Banks? They could, but we will see - in these pages - the astronomical price and their occult purposes.

The first step is to change our beliefs concerning money and its context, otherwise we risk to catch money with one arm and to push it away with the other one, and to cause an endless energy consumption and frustration as a consequence.

Let's now become familiar with money. Although I tried to explain everything in the easiest way possible, do not feel discouraged if you find some passages too technical, omit them and go on. Once finished this book, you will desire to resume them, bring into focus where we are and choose which opportunities to take.

Live this reading as a chat you have in front of a coffee break that you continue every time you like.

Once upon a time…

In the beginning, economy was based on trading, then, in the VII Century a.C., the first coins appeared both in Greece and Asia.

Golden and silver coins imposed on those made by other metals, such as iron or copper, due to the higher value of the material they were made of. This made them easy to carry around, since few coins represented high value. Moreover, since these metals were malleable, they could even be cut and used as fractions of the same coin.

In the XVI Century, in Europe, the goldsmiths offered to keep in storage the golden coins, in return for a receipt to the depositor. In this way money notes were put into circulation.

Those receipts guaranteed that in a certain "bank" a quantity of gold was stored and testified that the people who had them, owned the equivalent amount of gold. Each bank released its own notes; and that's the reason why they are also known as *"Bank…notes"*.

Each banknote gave the right to its possessor to exchange it, at any time, with the equivalent sum of gold, at the same bank that had released the note.

In a short time these receipts were welcomed as a matter of practicality.

Pretty soon, some goldsmiths based in London, noticed that there were always less people asking for gold in exchange of their receipts. For this reason, they began printing other receipts, for the same amount of gold stored and loan it in return for an interest. This maneuver let the goldsmiths earn arbitrarily on assets that did not exist, since they accounted the same asset more than once!

The consequence of this action was that the real stock of gold did not match the quantity of notes in the economic circuit, therefore the ration gold/bills got slowly lower at 50%; later on at 25% up to 3% of our days. But we will cover this topic in the next chapter.

Thanks to this technique, that was made official later on (incredible, right?) as *"fractional stock"*, all goldsmiths became bankers having high assets, since this operation made it possible to maneuver 4 times the assets they really had.

The economic power the goldsmiths acquired made them a hidden social and political entity that will be the explanation of many aspects of the present age.

This "technique" was immediately exported to the American colonies, before the American Civil War, and gave birth to the current American banking system and gradually even to ours.

Whilst these events were running in our continent, in 1536, less than 50 years after Cristoforo Colombo had found America, a Spanish mint in Mexico City coined the first silver coins of the "New World" and named them Dollar.

These coins reached the British colonies (America) too, but the British market policy was incline to keep the precious metals outside the American territory.

Thus the Spanish dollar, that was commonly divided into 8 pieces (named after this *"eight real coin"* despite it being only one dollar; and the quarter of dollar named *"two bits"*), became the unofficial currency.

To limit this phenomenon, the British banks, already extremely influential in all the world, made intense pressure to the British Parliament and managed to obtain votes for the *"Currency Act"* (1774), forcing all its colonies to use only English money from British banks.

This move made all the colonists lead towards British banks making them indebted, like all the British citizens!

In this way, all American settlers - already oppressed by British taxes - could only ask loans to the British Central bank and pay for interests too.

This gave birth to a reaction by American settlers that gave rise to the *"Boston Tea Party"* which lead to the American Independence war.

Later on, Benjamin Franklin declared: *"The refusal of King George III to authorize the colonies to operate with a "honest" monetary system that could free the individual from the pressure of money from the manipulators has possibly been the main cause of the revolution.". "The refusal of King George III to allow the colonies to operate an honest money system, which freed the ordinary man from the clutches of the money manipulators, was probably the prime cause of the Revolution."*

During the American Revolution, the colonies fought for their independence. Thus, every State decided to print out their "own" paper money to deal with the high military expenses, and for the same reason, the Continental Congress decided to print out its own money, known as *"continental currency"*.

In 1783 America gained its independence from England, but - later on - we will see that they could not defeat England's banking system.

During the war, each State, and the Congress too, input a high amount of notes into the system and, once the war was over, they had little to no value. Instead, who owned silver and gold coins was saved by the almost total devaluation.

To cope with this situation, in 1792, the Constitution of the United States was ratified and included the "Coniage Act" which denied the individual states the right to have their own currency, thus starting the era of the only American national currency: the dollar.

Coins were mint in gold and silver with the well-known American eagle printed on them. The golden coin had a value of 10 dollars.

In the meantime, in Europe, the new British banks, and their subsidiaries scattered in the various nations, had already taken control of the entire continent, thanks to the "Fractional Reserve" that allowed the banks to create money that did not exist and to benefit from the loan!

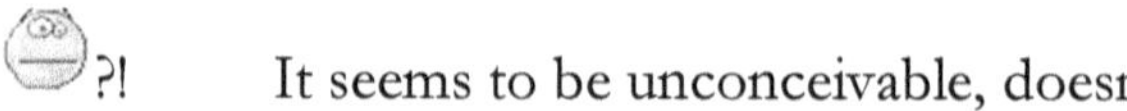?!   It seems to be unconceivable, doesn't it?

And yet it is like this and in the next chapter we will analyse how this could happen.

Fractional Reserve Banking

In other words: How banks "create" money...without even printing it!!!

To fully understand the entire western monetary system, we have to move to the United States of America because it is the starting point of its spread in the rest of the world, even though its origins are and always will be British (it is not a case that even nowadays London is considered to be the financial "capital city" of the world).

This recognition is not given for respect or tradition as you would think, because still now the real "banking intellighentia" of the entire western world is located there, and not in America, as we could believe.

Even this "secret" will be discussed later on...let's get back to the Fractional Reserve banking and to its "alchemy"!!!

The first question we should ask ourselves is *"How is it possible to create money without printing it?"*.

It is easy! It is sufficient to be the authorized entity to approve what it can and cannot be done and then approve anything that can serve its purpose!

I know this could seem like words placed together to create a sentence just to make people laugh, but unfortunately it is the most accurate explanation we can give on the Fractional Reserve banking system.

In the early days the "Federal Reserve" (established in 1913), developed a public text *"Modern Money Mechanics"* that even today is public - revised and updated - and that explains how the Fractional Reserve banking is a mean to "<u>create</u>" money. (!?)

It is unbelievable that this document really thinks to explain how to "create" money!!!

Here are some extracts from the original document:

Introduction:

"The purpose of this booklet is to describe the basic process of creating money in the banking system of "fractional reserve".

This approach shows the changes that occur in the balance sheets of banks when deposits in banks change as a result of monetary action by the Federal Reserve System - the central bank of the United States.

The relationships shown are based on simplified hypotheses. The relationships are shown as if they were mechanical, but they are not ..."

MODERN MONEY MECHANICS

A Workbook on Bank Reserves and Deposit Expansion

Federal Reserve Bank of Chicago

This complete booklet is was originally produced and distributed free by:
Public Information Center
Federal Reserve Bank of Chicago
P. O. Box 834
Chicago, IL 60690-0834
telephone: 312 322 5111
But it is now out of print. Photo copies can be made available by monques@myhome.net.

Introduction

The purpose of this booklet is to describe the basic process of money creation in a "fractional reserve" banking system. The approach taken illustrates the changes in bank balance sheets that occur when deposits in banks change as a result of monetary action by the Federal Reserve System - the central bank of the United States. The relationships shown are based on simplifying assumptions. For the sake of simplicity, the relationships are shown as if they were mechanical, but they are not. as is described

As already said above, the idea of the Fractional Reserve banking started after finding out that account holders did not withdraw the gold they deposited except a little percentage. For this same reason, at the beginning the goldsmiths - then the banks - took advantage of the permanent capital. At first they loaned a high percentage of the gold stored, keeping just the 50% of the reserve. Later on they realized the percentage could be lowered to 25% and in the 80s, they established that 3% of reserve was enough...

Below is the original document showing the minimum percentages of bank reserves required for both account holders and permanent capital that could also drop to *zero*!

Changes in Reserve Requirements

Thus far we have described transactions that affect the volume of bank reserves and the impact these transactions have upon the capacity of the banks to expand their assets and deposits. It is also possible to influence deposit expansion or contraction by changing the required minimum ratio of reserves to deposits.

The authority to vary required reserve percentages for banks that were members of the Federal Reserve System (member banks) was first granted by Congress to the Federal Reserve Board of Governors in 1933. The ranges within which this authority can be exercised have been changed several times, most recently in the Monetary Control Act of 1980, which provided for the establishment of reserve requirements that apply uniformly to all depository institutions. The 1980 statute established the following limits:

```
On transaction accounts
     first $25 million . . . . . . . . . 3%
     above $25 million . . . . . 8% to 14%

On nonpersonal time deposits . . . . 0% to 9%
```

The 1980 law initially set the requirement against transaction accounts over $25 million

What is even more intriguing is the section in the same paragraph:

"...FED's Governing Board can authorize the change of stock percentages at its discretion."

(?!)

On transaction accounts
first $25 million 3%
above $25 million . . . . . 8% to 14%

On nonpersonal time deposits . . . . 0% to 9%
The 1980 law initially set the requirement against transaction accounts over $25 million at 12 percent and that against nonpersonal time deposits at 3 percent. The initial $25 million "low reserve tranche" was indexed to change each year in line with 80 percent of the growth in transaction accounts at all depository institutions. (For example, the low reserve tranche was increased from $41.1 million for 1991 to $42.2 million for 1992.) In addition, reserve requirements can be imposed on certain nondeposit sources of funds, such as Eurocurrency liabilities.(18) (Initially the Board set a 3 percent requirement on Eurocurrency liabilities.)

The Garn-St. Germain Act of 1982 modified these provisions somewhat by exempting from reserve requirements the first $2 million of total reservable liabilities at each depository institution. Similar to the low reserve tranche adjustment for transaction accounts, the $2 million "reservable liabilities exemption amount" was indexed to 80 percent of annual increases in total reservable liabilities. (For example, the exemption amount was increased from $3.4 million for 1991 to $3.6 million for 1992.)

The Federal Reserve Board is authorized to change, at its discretion, the percentage requirements on transaction accounts above the low reserve tranche and on nonpersonal time deposits within the ranges indicated above. In addition, the Board may impose differing reserve requirements on nonpersonal time deposits based on the maturity of the deposit. (The Board initially imposed the 3 percent nonpersonal time

What does all this mean?

Making money...without printing it!

Let me explain: to simplify, just think of a reserve of 10% funds, which is more than three times the minimum authorized amount.

Depositing 100.000 euros, the bank has to keep as stock only 10.000 and it can use for loan 90.000, to which it will add interests since it is loaned money.

The person, or society, that benefits from the loan, will then give the money to a third party that will then deposit it in their own bank. At this point, in accounting terms, the 90.000 euros represent a possibility to be a "fractional" stock. Therefore, the new establishment has 9.000 euros as stock and the remaining 81.000 euros can be used for loans. This procedure can go on endless.

If we carry on with the calculation we find out that the 100.000 euros, that have been originally deposited, are generating interests on a actual sum of 900.000 euros!!!

It is <u>nine</u> times more than the original amount of money that the bank had, and this is only by calculating a stock of 10% and not 3%!

And here it is, the miracle: the money has been <u>created</u>!

It does not matter if that money does not really exist, the most important aspect is that, on an accounting basis, it has been input in the economics flow to "work" with its interests.

The most ironic part is that all this happens without anyone even printing the money. In fact, in the official FED document we can find:

"Clearly banks do not really pay the credits with the money they have received as deposits".

"<u>Clearly</u>" ?!

"<u>They do not really pay it</u>"?! 

It continues:

"If the really did it, there would not be the necessity to create more money. What they do when they make loans is to accept promissory notes in exchange for granted credits..."

banks together have $10,000 of deposits and reserves that they did not have before. However, they are not required to keep $10,000 of reserves against the $10,000 of deposits. All they need to retain, under a 10 percent reserve requirement, is $1000. The remaining $9,000 is "excess reserves." This amount can be loaned or invested. *See illustration 2.*

If business is active, the banks with excess reserves probably will have opportunities to loan the $9,000. <u>Of course, they do not really pay out loans from the money they receive as deposits. If they did this, no additional money would be created. What they do when they make loans is to accept promissory notes in exchange for credits to the</u> borrowers' transaction accounts. Loans (assets) and deposits (liabilities) both rise by $9,000. Reserves are unchanged by the loan transactions. But the deposit credits constitute new additions to the total deposits of the banking system. See *illustration 2.*

Oh well... Now we all feel cheered up and confident!

Luckily, as it is stated on the document, it is all so *"evident"*! 

The whole financial model is so perfectly masked that nobody can realize that the moment the Central Banks support loans to the nation, for the same reason, those billion of euros will be deposited by the above nation to the banks. Consequently, the banks, thanks to the Fractional Reserve banking system will increase up to nine times the original amount and it will be placed on the market as loans or other forms of investments.

We use to debate about the origins and reasons of the crisis!? Maybe even capturing the attention of the audience with elaborated explanations… leading to no benefit!

Plainly: every now and then all this "inexistent" money has to be eliminated, but we will talk about it further on.

This is a so "institutionalized" situation that even the Italian law states, with article 1834 of the Civil Code,:

"Depositing a sum of money in a bank, gives the bank the property of it [?!] and obliges it to give the same sum back after the expiry of the term limit or when asked by the depositor, in conformity of an appropriate length of time set by the parties or custom."

Therefore that money becomes, <u>in accordance with the law</u> (!) property of the bank that has to return it when the depositor asks for it.

How come "depositor"?

Of course, as long as the bank has the money, it is <u>its</u> money!

How can it be that all this system is made "legal"?

As we can find out in the next chapters, politics have always been serving the banking system and not vice versa. So much it is true that everything is in accordance with the law.

Did you know that in the event of bankruptcy state and banks are secure creditors "by law", and, only if the company assets are still available, the other creditors can proportionally be part of the distribution of the remaining money?

One more time, "in accordance with the law", they are discreetly the small amount of money still circulating in the economic flow.

Did you not notice?

Try asking the branch office of your bank for 5000 euros or 10000 euros cash... You will have to request it days in advance.

However, 8 years ago, you would encounter no problems with such a demand.

Today, with the pretext of a higher fiscal control, they are introducing the hypothesis to use nothing else but the credit card for all payments, just to get us used to it.

One more time, *"in accordance with law"*, banks can sell no longer gold.

Really, it seems no one realizes that the link between the client and its bank is merely virtual because it is no longer possible to access "physically" to anything that is property of the bank.

How is this possible?

I told you before:

Just be in charge of approving what can and what cannot be done and then... approve anything that can serve your own purpose!

The fact is that what happens is not due to necessity but it is just the way the politics - of whichever party - maneuver and realize the big plan.

The Fractional Reserve banking is the reason why impetuous economical cycles happen, followed by devastating bank crisis that wipe up the financial market.

This, too, will be explained about later on...

Inflation

We are now aware that a great opportunity the banks have is to increase virtually by ten times the money deposited, thanks to the fractional reserve banking and, later on, "selling" it in exchange of interests.

The money that the banks store, does not come exclusively from the citizens and/or firms. Big amounts of money come from the Central Banks (as the Federal Reserve, or the BCE), in fact only the central banks have the authority to introduce money in the economic flow, not the governments as we use to believe.

The fact is that the central banks do not give money free of charge but "sell" it to the banks and take their benefits from the interest rates, no matter if they are selling it to the banks or to the governments.

Basically, the circulating money introduced in the banking system generates a higher cost than its actual value, represented by the interests.

Therefore, the central banks input large quantities of money into the market, selling it to the banks in return for interests. The banks, then, have to sell this money at a higher price to have profit when they input it as investments and loans.

Here the economy starts again and, with it, also the inflation. As the word indicates, it creates an excess of money that decreases its value and causes a reduction of purchasing power per unit of money, therefore prices increase.

Inflation is the result of large monetary injections that has to make profits.

This explains clearly the equation: <u>The more is the input money, the higher is the debt</u>.

It does not matter if we refer to the public debt (when money goes to governments) or the private debt (when money is loaned to the citizens or firms) because the circulating money has an unique origin: the central bank that already asked and claims for interests on every single banknote.

For example, the table below shows the correlation between the money supply, the American national debt and the Consumers prices.

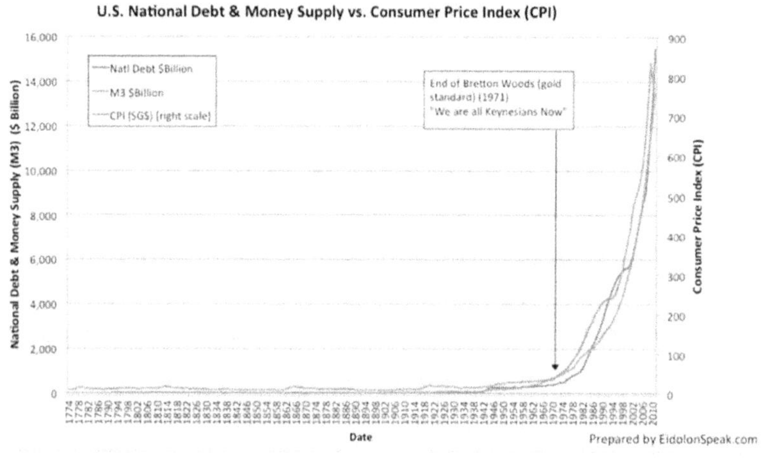

Since FED was born, 99 years ago, the dollar suffered a devaluation of 96%!

Behind the scenes

It is important to have understood that:

All the money placed on the market has always a higher cost than its innate value due to the interests.

It seems no one stops and thinks:

"If all the circulating money has at its origins some "interests", where does the money needed to pay off those interests come from, since the money placed in the market costs much more than its own value?"

Here we are! An inconvenient question people should not think about that reveals the most intriguing side of the great plan: to pay off the interests the debt cannot stay unchanged!

It is necessary to input more money.

This concept is fundamental to fully understand what will be explained in the next chapters:

Let's suppose to receive a loan of 100.000 euros and to have a 5% of interest rates per year. If we decide to pay only the interest rates, 5.000 euros per year would be the amount of money exiting our wallets. After 20 years we would have evened out our debt of 100.000 euros, but we should give the creditor his initial 100.000 euros back.

In the end, we would be returning double the initial loan. But where would the 100.000 euros extra come from if only the banks can use the "fractional reserve banking" and neither the people nor the states "make" money?

Can you understand it now?

There is no problem at all, you just get "other" money to pay the debt.

Think as per example of Italy that in 2012 had over 80 billion euros of debit interests. This means that, once paid the 80 billion euros, the following year the country should return another 80 billion, and so on.

But if we continue to give back multiples of 80 billion euros of interests, where do those billions come from?

From taxes. However, the taxes are paid by the people generating income, both salary or profit, and that money has its own "origin" and it is burdened with its "interests".

Who pays them?

This is why the States, each year, need further loans: to face the interests. In this way the interests themselves start to grow and the 80 billion euros are insufficient!

To make it clear for everybody: <u>If we could pay the debt with all the circulating money, there would still be a massive debt remaining!</u>

I think it is easy to understand that this system causes total dependence because it is <u>mathematically impossible to get out</u>!

Impossible!!!

This is the reason why inflation will always be a permanent feature, with ebb and flow trends, because "new" money will always be needed to pay the deficit created by the monetary system and caused by the interests of the circulating money.

This implies that bankruptcy is an intrinsic characteristic of the system, because if you put in the economic flow money with "added value" you will always have less money in circulation than the recorded amount with interests.

Remember: <u>the money inside a system is, and always will be, "less" than the recorded amount</u>.

The system is created so that it will never get better, on the contrary, it will always get worse!

The higher the debt, the higher will be the necessity to create new money, thus creating, again, a higher debt.

Checkmate!

Most of us do not realize that many nations - included Italy - offer, as a solution to face debts, the "privatization" of the government's real estate. In other words, the government sells part of its real estate to privates in exchange of money, to reduce the debt.

I hope you see that this is an illusion: once again, alibi to impoverish the states and benefit selected few.

This financial model does not give any escape hatch, therefore it is useless selling anything to pay a part of the debt (even though nobody could extinguish its own debt) because it would just postpone the moment the current debt will increase.

More and more economists are saying that in the next decades more than 60% of the nations will go bankrupt due to something called "debt".

All this is happening because of some "people" that cut the knees to the entire planet and made us accept that banknotes must be printed by private authority, to which we have to pay "interests".

Isn't it incredible?

In the next pages we will reveal every secret. It will be an interesting reading, I promise you.

The most frightening aspect of all this is that the money that the banks loan is not even "equivalent to", in other words something equivalent to... To what?

It does not exist!

It is only an invention perpetrated by the Fractional Reserve or the decision of a Central Bank that do not input real money in circulation as it seems to be. Unluckily we go bankrupt if we do not fulfill our debts or our mortgage!

How can this falsity be professed or, even worse, how can it be legalized?!

Surprise!

The whole banking system is PRIVATE OWNED!

Maybe not everybody knows that FED ("Federal Reserve Bank", or even the BCE (Central European Bank), or any other banking institute, are not governmental institutes, but <u>PRIVATE</u> OWNED firms!

They are all connected to the FED, but we will find this out at the end.

The management of these institutes is not chosen by the governments or the politicians, but by ordinary citizens; if anything, it is true the contrary: politicians are controlled by the banking system!

The institutes give notice of the people elected as chief executive and call them "governors" - even if they do not relate to governments – to let people perceive them as public officials...

This also applies to some definitions, for example the names:

The name *"Federal Reserve Bank"* was chosen to puzzle people and let them think of a "federal" institute, but it is just a <u>private</u> firm.

So the *"Central European Bank"* that leads people to think about a bank "super partes" representing all Europe ...

Same with Bankitalia!

The Central Banks are _extra-governmental_ organisations and, therefore, are not subject to budget review or whichever auditing activity!

The Central Banks simply make a self-certification of their accounts.

 ?!

The Central Banks have officially two jobs: keep under control interest rates and inflation.

Inflation originates from the introduction of money in the market.

This is their "official" role.

The Central Banks do not print money on behalf of the governments but they loan it to the governments and make them fall into debt. In fact, the loaned money has an added value given by the interests - as we have seen earlier – and there will never be enough circulating money to return the amount with the interests.

We are trapped in a vicious circle.

The Central Banks decide arbitrarily how much money to print according to their "own" criteria about the economic stability.

The Central Banks control and set the value of their money by increasing or decreasing the availability of it.

Can you see, it seems so easy to understand and in favour of the citizens, and yet not only this system does not work properly but it gets worse as the years pass by: globalisation (the introduction of more countries into this system) expanded the problem into vast boundaries. If you take a closer look, you will find out that the countries affected are those inside this system and not the ones outside it!

All this should definitely make a doubt grow inside of people.

The position of the western banking institutes is so independent and free from obligation that anything they approve must be solely accepted.

Even if we use to think the banknotes represent the amount of the circulating money, we can touch and use only 3% of the real amount of money that is in the system. The remaining 97% are just "bit" inside of a computer.

Each banknote that has been physically printed has its own personal value given <u>by the same banking system</u> that printed it.

The purple paper refers to 500 euros value, the yellow to 200 euros, the green to 100 euros, and so on. Regardless of the colour of the paper, the total cost the bank faces is approximately 15/20 cent per banknote.

On the other hand, the task of the realization of the coins, that have a much higher production cost than banknotes (since the value of the metals is higher than the value of paper), has been devolved to the mints of the countries.

This happens both in American and Italy, in fact, on the Banca d'Italia official website (remember it is a private institute and it is not governmental) it is stated:

BANKNOTES AND COINS

The "Banca d'Italia" emits banknotes in euros based on the accords took in the Eurosystem.

Within the Eurosystem, the Banca d'Italia produces the amount of euro banknotes allocated to it, inputs the banknotes in the economic flow and provides for the removal and replacement of deteriorated bills, participates in the activity of study and experimentation of new safety features for the bills. It contributes to the determination of the production quantities and of common guidelines regarding the actions against forgery.

<u>Coins in Italy are mint by the Istituto Poligrafico e Zecca of the country on behalf of the Ministero dell'Economia e delle Finanze that distributes the coins to the country with the help of branches of the Banca d'Italia.</u>

Not bad, right?

Nobody, though, wonders where the golden stock has gone ...

In December 2010, the "public" census of the worldwide classification (!) of stock of gold placed among the first six positions:

BCE with 10.784 tons of gold

FED with 8.133 t

Deutsche Bundesbank *(together with the BCE)* with 3.396 t

FMI with 2.814 t

Bankitalia *(together with the BCE)* with 2.451 t

Banque de France *(together with the BCE)* with 2.435 t

If we would be less distracted by the media, we could also ask ourselves:

How is all this possible?

How and when did all this happen?

Who "invented" it and is using it to benefit himself?

Let's go find out. To do so, though, we have to travel back in time to Europe and discover why London is - still today - considered as the worldwide financial capital city.

I assure you that it will be more engaging and captivating than you could imagine and <u>who says this is a person that has never been fond of history</u>.

I guarantee it!

With just a bit of attention we can have access to the "secret code" of our times and, therefore, we can analyse things better and have a "pre...view" of various things...

Unfortunately the secret code is concealed inside our history and the continual fabrication of it, but do not be afraid to discover a bit of history because I promise, again, that it will be breathtaking.

Being aware of the origins of the great plan, and therefore the entire philosophy behind it, will let us understand certain circumstances in advance and take proper measures before the winter comes and afflicts our the society.

Frankfurt-am-Main:

the roots

Mozes Amschel Bauer, a wealthy "goldsmith" who loaned money, in 1744 settled in a ghetto in Frankfurt-am-Main, his native city (it is important to remember this city). Amschel had a child: Mayer Amschel Bauer who changed his family name later on in Rothschild. It was him that gave birth to the Rothschild dynasty with the aid of the "House of Rothschild".

Mayer started with his social success at the loyal service of Prince William that, during his confinement in Denmark, named Mayer as guardian of his immeasurable fortune.

Mayer had five children. He sent them in five different capital cities to expand the financial activity of the family. The cities were: London Frankfort, Vienna, Naples and Paris.

The most prominent children were those sent to London and Paris (we will discover this also in the American Independence war).

In 1807, Nathan Mayer Rothschild (1777-1836) founded in London "N.M. Rothschild", the family bank.

In that period the Rothschild family was already so influent in all Europe that Nathan venture to say publically:

"I do not care about the puppets they choose to rule England. Whoever controls the flow of money in Britain's capital city, controls Britain. And I am the one in charge of the flow of money in England"

Nathan Mayer Roththschild

To fully understand what Nathan has stated we need to travel back to that era, when the Royal Family was Britain's maximum expression of power and respect. The newest member of the financial world dare publicly call *"puppets"* the Royal Family members, without any consequences.

The public disrespect towards the crown and the Royal Family is the demonstration of how powerful the Rothschild family had become in all Europe.

When Nathan Mayer died, he devised some "rules" that still nowadays guide the family:

(1) All key positions in the "Rothschild Home" must be held by family members and not subordinates.

Only the male members of the family are authorised to participate in the family business.

The head of the family is the older son, unless the majority of the family decides otherwise.

It is for this reason that Nathan, who was an intelligent person, was named as head of the Rothschild Home in 1812.

(2) The family must maintain the enormous fortune with marriages between first or second degree cousins.

This rule has been strictly followed in the beginning but, later on, when the other rich Jew bankers descendants made the scene, softened and some members of the Rothschild family were allowed to marry selected members of the new elite group.

(3) Amschel warned his heirs against any public inventory, or whatever else, made by the court of his properties. He forbid, too, any legal action to give forth the value of the inheritance.

Ignoring these dispositions and acting in conflict with them entailed the exclusion of the member from the hereditary tree.

(4) Rothschild planned to sustain all the members of the family, granting all the women, their husbands and their children a perpetual income, on the condition that only the male member took care of it.

(5) Whoever questions this pact would lose his family rights.

This last provision has been specifically studied to shut the mouths of whoever could break the relationship between the members of the family.

Rothschild, obviously, knew that there were many family secrets that had never to be told.

The winning factors of the "House of Rothschild" were:

Complete secrecy on all commercial activity carried out by the family.

An incredible capacity to foresee the events and use them for their benefit. The whole family has been driven by a never ending desire of power and wealth.

Pure cruelty in all business relationships.

Evidently these rules have been passed on correctly since this family is still nowadays unknown to the media world. No news at all about them!

The biographer Frederic Morton, in *"The fabulous Rothschild"*, writes that Mayer Amschel Rothschild and his five children were financial wizards, moved by a "diabolical pulsation" to reach success in all their secret venture.

We will, in fact, find out in the following pages that their success has no equals in the entire history of our planet!

Lionel de Rothschild (1808-1879) that was the head of London's bank branch, became the first Jew member of Britain's parliament history, whereas Nathaniel de Rothschild (1804-1915) became the first noble of the Rothschild family, acquiring, in 1885, the status of Baron. He was the first Jew of the House of Lords.

In the nineteenth century the Rothschild family had an " unconditioned" power in the continent. A power that nobody could resist.

But they were still "weak" in America.

To America, lads!

The Rothschild family began their expansion in America by supporting both sides during the Independence war. In this way they would benefit from both sides and come out as a winner regardless of how the war would have ended.

Lionel, from England, supported the northern states. On the other side, his brother, James, supported the southern states from France.

Their expansion goal aimed to acquire the American Central Bank.

Unfortunately they encountered, several times, the opposition of President Lincoln.

Lincoln was particularly famous for his battles against the banking system and adverse to the heavy interests the British banks were demanding. He created an independent currency without added interest rates, a currency that would not create a "debt", the well-known "*Greenback-dollar*". In 1862 it became the national currency.

Lincoln stated: "*It is the biggest blessing the americans could ever have, since it gave America and its citizens freedom from the banks*".

This choice was not well-accepted by the powerful and shameless English and American banking world. For this reason Lincoln stated:

"I have got two enemies, the South of the country in front of me and the banks behind me. The enemy I fear most is represented by the banks!"

Exhausted by the continuous tensions with the whole banking system, Lincoln tried a compromise with the "eastern" bankers.

The "*New York Times*", whose owner, Leonard Jerome, was closely related with the British and Austrian banking oligarchy, publicly supported the approval of the "National Bank Act" and published, on the 21st May, 1863, a letter from McCulloch who offered himself as the "controller" of the above legislation.

McCulloch is elected as Treasure Secretary in March 1865 by Lincoln for the role he could play as a mediator with the banking institutes.

The next month, as the war was ending, Lincoln was assassinated...

Soon after Lincoln's homicide, McCulloch and his international allies attacked the economic program of the ex-president.

Obstinacy and grit!

The Rothschild's family history had been symptomatic of obstinacy and grit in pursuing its expansion. No wonder, then, if they launched another attack to acquire the main bank of America.

This time, though, they use a less "direct" tactic: they planned a partnership between *Kuhn Loeb & Co."*, the bank with which the family had business in America and Jacob Schiff; later on, introduced also the two brothers Felix e Paul Warburg. All of them were heirs of wealthy Jew bankers' families coming from Frankfurt-am-Main and strictly related to the Rothschild family business.

As still now *"Kuhn Loeb & Co."* is not an institute on which is posed much attention but it is really influent (it acts behind the scenes in the financial world and in FED) and Schiff and Warburg are two dynasties among the most powerful in the world, it is useful to learn its background.

Newsweek (1.2.1936) reports a short story about Kuhn Loeb & Co.:

"At the beginning, in 1850, Abraham Kuhn and Solomon Loeb were merchants of different goods in Lafayette, Indiana.

As it usually happened in those new growing areas, the majority of the transactions were on a credit basis. They soon found themselves bankers.

In 1867, in New York City, they founded the investment bank "Kuhn Loeb & Co." and began doing so good business with the Rothschild family as to take Jacob Schiff as partner.

Jacob was a young man who spent a lot of time at the House of Rothschild and consequently, was in contact with the European financial world.

He married Therese Loeb and, ten years after the beginning of his partnership with Kuhn, Loeb & Co., Jacob became head of the company.

Under Jacob's charge, the interchanges between Europe and American became more profitable for everybody. In fact, "Kuhn & Loeb" became the <u>second bank of all United States of America</u>, after J.P.Morgan.

(Notice that the first bank remained J.P.Morgan)

Jacob became a millionaire at that time and financed the American railways, the growth of the Western Union, Westinghouse, keeping a notable shareholding in these businesses.

A "flagship" was financing to the end Carnegie steel plants, making Andrew Carnegie a lucky 298 billion dollar man at that time.

The same he did with "Standard Oil" making John Rockefeller a 318 billion dollar man at that time.

On the 30th of November 1999, the Standard Oil, that merged with Exxon e Mobil and affiliated with Imperial Oil - operating in Canada - became *"ExxonMobil"*, <u>the biggest company in the whole world for sales volume!</u>

The connection between all these families is, still nowadays, very strong. We will know more about it later on, let's now get back to that era...

The role of "Kuhn & Loeb" in the above mentioned transactions used to be so relevant that Jacob was able to exercise control in all the companies such as the *"National City Bank of New York"*, the *"Equitable Life Assurance Society"*, in *"Wells Fargo & Company"*, and in

"Union Pacific Railroad".

In 1917 Lev Davidovich Bronshtein - also known as "Leon Trotsky" - considered the father of the Russian revolution, was exiled in New York and there he met Jacob Schiff.

As the "New York Journal" of 3.2.1949 says, the nephew of Jacob Schiff, Jhon stated to Cholly Knickerbocker, a journalist, that his grandfather gave 20 million dollars to help the triumph of communism in Russia.

(If you are passionate of history I suggest you to read "My Life" by Trotsky).

The involvement of American finance during the Russian revolution was not only restricted to Schiff but also concerned the *"Chase National Bank"* owned by the <u>Rockefellers</u>. Shortly after it merged with the *"Manhattan Bank"*, property of the <u>Warburg family, and </u>consolidated in the *"Chase Manhattan Bank"*, the Standard Oil - owned by the Rockefeller family - acquired 50% of the Caucasian area, nationalized by the soviets at the end of the revolution, built a refinery and sealed an agreement of supply with Europe.

The transaction included a loan of 75 million dollar to the soviets.

(Prof. A. Sutton "Standford University Hoover Institute" in "The role of devil in human revolution" of David Ash)

It is not just coincidence that, out of 384 commissioners forming the Russian government, <u>264 came from the United States of America</u>.

(Robert Wilton, "London Times" April 1918)

So, these transactions gave the opportunity to the Rothschild family to deeply settle down in the American economy and if the goal to acquire one of the biggest American bank had gone beyond... now they could reach the <u>entire</u> American banking system.

In the meantime, in1897, Jacob Schiff, head of the "Kuhn & Loeb", made a partnership with Felix <u>Warburg</u>, coming from a wealthy family of Frankfurt-am-Main connected with the Rothschild family.

Five years later, in 1902, Paul Warburg – brother of Felix - became a partner of the "Kuhn & Loeb" and married the other daughter of Salomon Loeb: Nina (he became Jacob Schiff's brother in law).

The main purpose of having Paul in America was to influence the Congress to make a law and create a "Central" bank in charge to make money.

The origin of FED

At the beginning of the twentieth century, the whole American banking marketplace was ruled by the Rothschild, J.D. Rockefeller, J.P. Morgan, Warbrug e Schiff families.

They were <u>eventually</u> able to force through the legislature and found their <u>own</u> *"Central Bank"*.

In 1910 Paul Warburg, in a a speech to the nation, suggested to establish only one "Federal Bank" with 100 million dollars, that would have the assignment to emit money *(what for us today means : <u>having more debt</u>!)*.

As the proposal seemed to have caused as many reactions among the people as if it had not been made one, the same year, J.P.Morgan gathered in a secret meeting 6 representatives of the high finance in *Jekyll Island* to redefine America's economic structure.

The meeting lasted 10 days, including the "Thanksgiving Day" (it is so relevant for them to be compared to Christmas Day) that was celebrated away from the families. (The meeting was discovered years later and it is nowadays public knowledge).

Among the people present at the meeting, were Paul Warburg *(also representing the Rothschild empire)* and William Rockefeller.

The purpose of the meeting was to capitalise on the latest crisis, to create a <u>private</u> Central Bank.

To go by unnoticed, it was decided to choose another name rather than "bank". The word "bank" was perceived negatively since the banks were responsible for the great crisis. Therefore, it was decided to change the word "bank" with "reserve". "Reserve" was reassuring, it communicated confidence to the citizens. For the same reasons above, the word "central" was replaced with "federal", allowing people to think of something that came from the government instead of privates.

These were the bases that three years later led up to the *"Federal Reserve Act"*, from which the Federal Reserve was found!

To strengthen the idea it was necessary to have a single Central Bank, as Warburg suggested, the lords of finance asked the Congress to investigate the causes for the collapse of economy. Senator Nelson Aldrich, strictly linked to the banking system - he married a woman belonging to the Rockefeller family - was in charge of the investigation and ... guess what? <u>The board approved to have a sole Central Bank which the entire banking system had to refer to with the objective to prevent other economic crisis .</u>

In 1913 *Thomas Woodrow Wilson* was elected president of the United States of America, thanks to the support of the banking community.

His election, though, withstood with a "compromise". In return for the support he had received during the elections, he had to approve the *"Federal Reserve Act"*.

Pay real attention now, starting with the date:

December 23, 1913, two days before Christmas, when more than half of the senators were on holiday, the Senate approved the founding principles of the "Federal Bank" and, therefore, the "Federal Reserve Act" thanks to the majority of votes.

What happened next needs no explanation: for the first and only time in America's history, exactly one hour after the Senate had voted the constitution of the Federal Bank, President Woodrow Wilson signed the "Federal Reserve Act" making it irrevocable and operational . All this happened <u>after just one hour and on Christmas eve</u>!

After years of a meticulous planning , in a single day (pay attention to the names) Rothschild, JP Morgan, City Bank of Bynn, Loeb & Co (former "Kuhn and Loeb") were in control of <u>all American economy</u>!

What happened from that day onwards is reflected throughout history...until our days!

What is funny is that it is not over, it will never be, at least in the century!

Few but...

Although, at that time, J.P. Morgan was considered one of the richest men in America, it has been discovered, at his death, that it was a lieutenant of the Rothschilds.

J.P. Morgan owned only 19% of his firm, that was <u>controlled by the Rothschild family</u>!

It is understandable by now, that the whole American economy was completely controlled by the FED: few people closely tied in with each other.

From the moment the act was effective, the American economy started a fluctuating pace and this system was imported also in our continent, producing the same kind of consequences!

It is now time to understand why this happened, what the benefits are and, especially, who benefits ...

We have previously seen what originates inflation: an intense inflow of money that, from the above events on, is private.

First example:

In 5 years, from 1914 to 1919, the FED doubled the flow of money, loaning it to many smaller banks *(money auction sales)*.

In 1920, the FED called back the credits , forcing the small banks to pay their debts. These small banks, though, had been using the money putting it into the market *(money auction sales)*

As a consequence economy collapsed *(as in 1907)* and more than 400 banks bankrupted.

Charles Lindbergh stated: *"With the FED's deed, panic can be created with a simple mathematical equation."*!

Second example:

From 1921 to 1929, the FED increased by 62% the circulating money ... this means again accessible credits

Moreover, this fact created *"Margin setting"* in the finance world: a loan 10 times more the assets with the clause of return in 24 hours!

A few months before the black October 1929, Rockefeller, Bernard Barak and other *"insiders"* quit the stock market and, once again, the FED called back the loaned assets.

This time, as the banking system was rapidly expanding, more and 16'000 banks went bankrupt, not to say thousands of companies.

(Does this activity remind you something ?)

In this occasion, though, the FED pulled back the money instead of putting it in circulation.

Senator *Louis McFadden* of the Congress, made a speech declaring FED's responsibilities. After trying to assassinate him twice, and failing both times, he was poisoned before he could carry out his cause.

At that time the , banks could input into the market only the amount of money equivalent to their stocks of gold. When the biggest depression than ever occurred, they took advantage of the situation and regain the bubble the Fractional Reserve had done.

A colossal procedure of collecting all the gold and redefine its price was carried out.

By now, pay close attention...

To awaken the economy, using the crisis as an excuse, in April 1933 it was promulgated a law , called *"Gold Caesar"*, approved by President Roosevelt. The law stated that, from May the 1st 1933 (25 days after the approval), all citizens had to deposit all the gold they possessed – coins, bars or just the certificates - to the FED or the banks connected.

Whoever was found having gold would be punished with 10 years of prison.

Once collected all the gold, which at that time had the price of 20 dollars per ounce, Roosevelt officially established its price in 35 dollars the following year and authorised the re-introduction into the market !

This manoeuvre increased FED's stocks of gold at no cost - because people has been obliged to give its gold - and also increased the price of the gold itself by 117% in just one year.

I almost forgot: the gold had become "private", <u>property of the Federal Reserve.</u> In fact, together with the law *"Gold Caesar"*, the dollars, that originally carried the writing of its similar value in silver or gold, from 1933 on lost this indication

In the image below, we can see two banknotes of the same value. But if we look closer, we will notice that the one belonging to 1928 displays "Silver Certificate" whilst the banknote of 1936 displays "Federal Reserve Note".

Moreover, the 1928 dollar displays a blue print on the left that "certifies" that the banknote can be traded for the equivalent sum of gold/silver.

The *"new"* dollar has a value of...?!

Obviously, the value negotiated. Well, who negotiated the value?

The FED, of course!

The banking and monetary situation was such a muddle that Henry Ford *(Ford Motor Company)* wrote:

"It is a luck that the citizens of our nation do not understand our banking and monetary system. If they did I think there would be a revolution no later than tomorrow morning".

Thomas Jefferson, the President of the United States stated:

"I think that banks are more dangerous to us than an entire army. They cre-

ated an economic aristocracy that subdues our government.

The increasing power of money should be took away from the banks and given back to the citizens".

Paul Warburg, years after, on the 17 of February 1950 stated, refering to the Senate of the United States:

"We will have a worldwide control, like it or not. The only question is if this control will be the result of the citizens' approval or the result of the conquest".

As already said, what causes the value of money is the quantity of it circulating into the market and the FED *(the BCE is the equivalent in Europe)* decides how much money to input and if it is the case.

The above system is so well entrenched that nobody can oppose this scheme, except countries like Iceland where its citizens voted for the cancellation of public debt towards the banks. Obviously, this has happened because with a worldwide picture, a small country with 319'000 inhabitants passes unnoticed.

In June 1963, John F. Kennedy, firmly against the authority of the banks, as president, decided to sign the *"Executive Order 11.110".* This gave the American government the power to print notes in relation with the amount of stocks of gold the country owned, as *article I, section 8 of the Constitution* expected. <u>This tactic would avoid further debts from interests, ignoring the presence of the FED.</u>

In the following months, J.F. Kennedy input approximately $4.3 million dollars in the market, together with the already existing money of the FED. This money was <u>property of the United States</u>.

On November 22, 1963, just a few months after this decision and after a <u>dramatic</u> speech to inform the citizens about what was continuosly happening behind the scenes *(you will find the transcript further on),* J.F.K. was assassinated.

Here are two bills of the same year with two different "sources".

J.F. Kennedy act was cancelled on September 9, 1987 with the executive order 12.608 by President Reagan.

The motive was: *"Elimination of executive orders and of technical adjustments to simplify the system".*

 *?!*

A few "diversifications"

The "Central Banks" have another way to enrich themselves: wars.

During wars, countries necessitate to have rapidly access to a high supply of money and, of course, during the negotiations whoever has the money benefits of the situation *(law of supply and demand)*.

Since 1913, there have been several wars. The most important were World War 1, World War 2 and the Vietnam War.

We'll find out later how everything has always at the base the same origin , the same ideologies and the political reasons are just a façade.

World War 1

World War 1 was at first a European countries' business. In fact, President Wilson declared America "neutral", but the on going of the war was causing relevant <u>financial</u> difficulties to the allies!

So, a pretext to join the allies had to be searched.

According to what Edward House wrote in his book: *"The Intimate Papers of Colonel House"*, in which are gathered several documents regarding the period of time from 1912 to 1919, in a private conversation, British Ministry of Foreign Affairs, Edward Grey, asked President's Wilson advisor, colonel Edward House:

"What would happen if the Germans sank a cruise ship with American passengers on board?"

House answered:

"National outrage, and this could be enough to start a war".

The Americans gave great media coverage of the forthcoming trip of the cruise ship Lusitania that would sail from New York to Liverpool.

When the Germans were notified that the Lusitania would have navigated in the middle of a war zone, bringing resources to the allies, they tried to discourage the passengers to embark and bought 50 issues on American newspapers to inform the Americans it could have been a trip extremely dangerous .

As soon as the Americans knew about the German campaign on their newspaper to boycott the mission, the 50 issues were banned for alleged "bureaucratic reasons". They succeeded in stopping the printing of all but one.

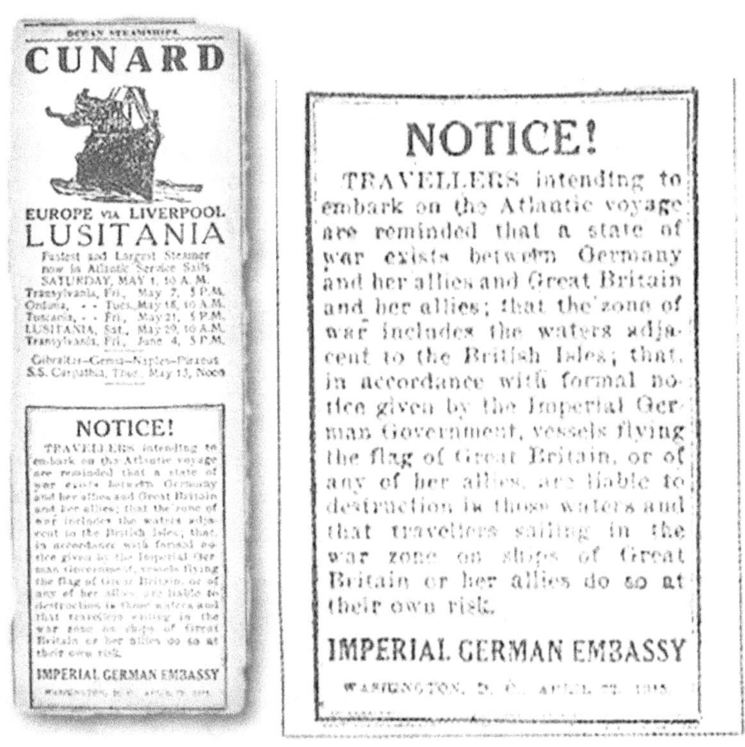

On May 7, 1915, the "Lusitania" was deliberately sent to the German waters . It was clear that the U-Boots would have attacked, and so they did, sinking the ship.

This marked the beginning of the governmental "propaganda" that made the damage suffered as its epicentre. The cities were invaded by poster resembling the damage suffered, with the aid of images that would urge the public opinion.

Both English and American governments tried to keep the facts hidden . It was immediately forbidden to do scuba diving in the area where the Lusitania sank and this prohibition lasted since a recent past .

At the time, a lot of discussion was made on the mysterious question : did the British decode or not the German military message , so they knew the exact position of the U-Boot?

The following document: *"Zimmerman telegram"*, proves that the British had decoded the German messages , therefore they knew the position of the U-Boot.

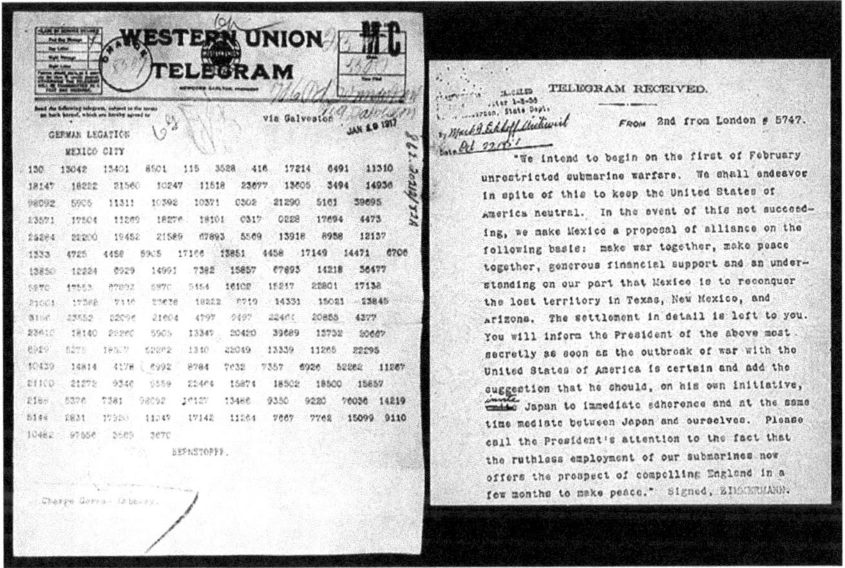

In the postwar, the English army went several times in the place the Lusitania sank for military "exercises" with anti-submarine mines (id est depth mines).

Nevertheless, in July 2006, Victor Quirke's "Cork Sub Aqua Club" found, along with several weapons, 15,000 belts of 303 bullets each, when, instead of it 90 tons of crates/boxes "sealed" of ... butter, as it was known !   (?!)

As a "consequence" of sinking the Lusitania, American joined the war and 323.000 Americans died.

It is estimated that J.D. Rockefeller benefitted of 200 million dollars from the war.

The war required 30 billion dollars that were loaned by the FED... with interests!

World War 2

World War 2 began, for the Americans, with the attack to Pearl Harbor (December 7, 1941)

Robert Stinnett, journalist, researcher of World War 2 and author of the book/documentary *"The truth about FDR and Pearl Harbor"*, spent 16 years looking in the state and military archives, producing over 200.000 documents and carrying out nearly a hundred interviews...

His final thesis, that can be put together with many others, is documented in detail: the attack to Pearl Harbor had been known several months in advance by the American government and it had been "sustained" by President Roosevelt, who belonged to a family of bankers since the 18th Century and had an uncle working in the FED.

Roosevelt needed a motive to join the war, but, for the "public opinion", it was best to be looked at as "victims" of an attack rather than as the "attackers", exactly what happened with the Lusitania!

There are several internal documents that prove that Roosevelt had been teasing Japan since 1939 to attack America. The Americans, on the other side, were against attacking Japan and the Japanese were not interested in America's provocation because they were concentrating on Asia.

The document the proved what has just been said is the *"Internal-memo"* by McCollum written on October 7, 1940, one year before the attack to Pearl Harbor.

Although the entire 5 pages document is a summery of economic and political tactics, page 3 ends with:

"If for these motives Japan can be induced to attack us, much better. In any scenery we must be ready to accept the threat of war".

The document that follows has the related sentence underlined.

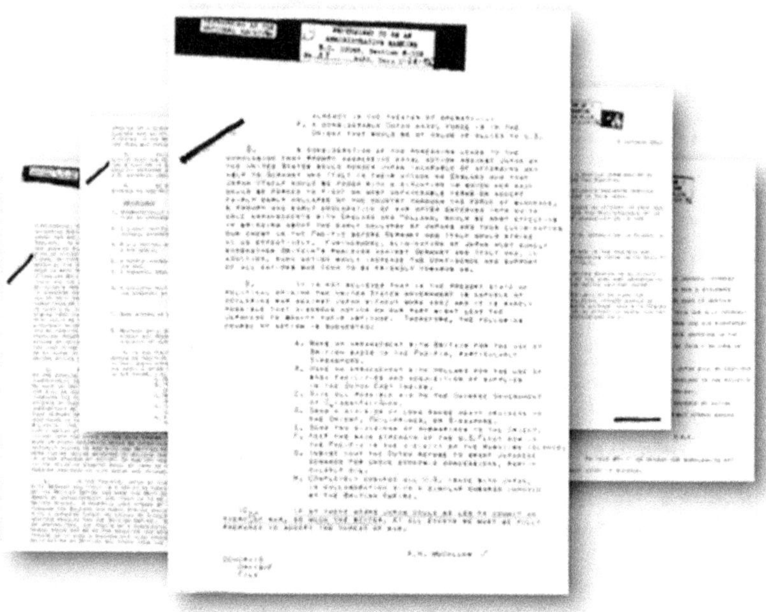

Roosevelt interrupted any commercial relationship America had with Japan, froze Japanese's assets, supported their enemies, although this was against the international war laws.

Then he moved the American fleet His next move has been to move the whole american army near Japan, in the warm waters of Hawaii...

On October 12, a marine military report alerted the government of a high quantity of Japan's military means moving toward Pearl Harbour ...

Half way into November 1941, few weeks before the attack,

Roosevelt sent an order to all commanders in Pearl Harbor that said: "The United States would appreciate Japan to be responsible of the first act of war".

Three days before the attack, the Australian *intelligence* informed Roosevelt of a big Japanese military formation near Pearl Harbor. Roosevelt did nothing and 2400 soldiers lost their lives.

Prior to the attack, 83% of the Americans did not want to go to war. After the attack, one million volunteered!

Other ideas on the "war business":

During the Nazi period, I.G.Farben produced 85% of Germany's explosives and gas for the extermination camps.

One of its partners was *"Standard Oil Co"* owned by Rockefeller. In fact, the German airplanes could not work without a patented additive of "Standard Oil Co".

The devastating bombardment on London was made possible for the Germans, thanks to the 20 million dollar investment of the I.G.Farben products.

New York's *"Union Banking Corporation"* has been constantly in in collusion with Nazis and in fact it was discovered that they had high amounts of money belonged to the Nazis in their deposits.

Who was the president at the time? Prescott Bush, father of George Bush and grandfather of George W. Bush!

The lucrative involvement of the Bush family with the nazis is no more a secret and is, nowadays, profusely documented.

The Vietnam War

The Vietnam War - in 1965 - was an epochal war originated as a reaction to the attack launched at two American destroyers from Northern Vietnam .

This attack, though, has never been proven of!

Robert McNamara, the Defence Secretary, soon after stated that it had been an "error" and many other officials stated that it was a lie.

The Vietnam War has been one of the most "expensive" for America: more than 59'000 American soldiers died and more than 300'000 were injured; but the "costs" that the money business had were not these.

This war was a conflict that politics did not want to cease: it lasted 10 long years, from 1965 to 1975!!!

Gulf of Tonkin, the public opinion (as always in the politics' objectives) is informed that two destroyers, *"Maddox"* and *"Turner Joy"*, the two battleships assigned to the surveillance mission called *"Desoto"*, were under attack...

On August 5, with the pretext of revenge, the never-ending Vietnam War started with a mission - named *"Pierce Arrow"* - that considered at first aerial attacks.

A few years later , <u>thanks to the internal documents of the Penta-</u>

gon and for the outing of the officials, it would disclose the *"Turner Joy"* had never been under attack.

Moreover, the *"Maddox"* was attacked by one missile (14.5 millimetres of length) shot by one of the three Northern Vietnamese Torpedo as a matter of fact, but it was the reaction to the attack ordered by the Captain of the *"Maddox"* John J. Herrick that shot three times first.

The 4 F-Crusaders that took off to help the Maddox damaged two of the three Torpedo's and sank the other one. The Maddox returned to America without further problems, without deaths. For this reason, President Lundon Johnson commented on the situation to the Secretary of State : *"Those sailors could have been firing at flying fishes"*.

It is now public knowledge that the beginning of the Vietnam war was "fabricated" so that shortly after The New York Times wrote an article stating that there had not been any "attack".

The New York Times

Asia Pacific

Records Show Doubts on '64 Vietnam Crisis

President Lyndon B. Johnson cited the attacks to persuade Congress to authorize broad military action in Vietnam, but historians in recent years have concluded that the Aug. 4 attack never happened.

Here is the beginning of one of the longest, "lucrative", war ever fought.

Who knows!

Well, there are not only wars. For example, what about September 11?

Dunno?! It must be said that it seems to present a much similar clichè...

It is now known that among the governmental environments rumors about an imminent attack had been already spreading.

Furthermore, despite being aware of this threat, the first authority in the world came under attack in broad daylight, right at its heart: New York and after an hour the air defence had not yet taken off ... Leaving Flight 77 free to hit the Pentagon.

Not to mention the various remarks which no one has ever given official response to, such as the fact that it is scientifically proven that titanium turbines may NOT melt at temperatures that would be created in a potential impact. This means that we would have to find the remains of the clash, but it seems that nothing has ever been found..

 ?!

The conduct of Dick Cheney (former vice-president of the United States at that time) on the morning of September 11 supports the theory of a high military command with the order: "do not take off." '

The deposition given to the "9/11 Commission," of the Secretary of Transportation Norman Mineta, describes the scene happened in the underground bunker of the White House, on the morning of September 11 :

"During the time that the airplane (Flight 77) was coming into the Pentagon, there was a young man who would come in and say to the Vice President…the plane is 50 miles out…the plane is 30 miles out….and when it got down to the plane is 10 miles out, the young man also said to the vice president "do the orders still stand?" And the Vice President turned and whipped his neck around and said "Of course the orders still stand, have you heard anything to the contrary!??"

In short, no one will ever know what really happened, but for sure there are countless public statements and also affidavit , which help raise "some doubts"...

Not to say about really weird facts: maybe someone ignores that the total number of towers that collapsed is three. The third tower fell down late in the afternoon - 7 hours after the attack - because it was demolished.

Before drawing conclusions, it is essential to know other facts:

Look at the following map, it is fundamental to understand that only the twin towers collapsed (WTC-1 e WTC-2) whereas the 3 adjacent towers (WTC-3, -4 e -6) were just damaged. They were demolished later on together with the fifth tower.

Pay, then, close attention to the position of the other tower that would explode 7 hours later, WTC-7, as a consequence of the incident.

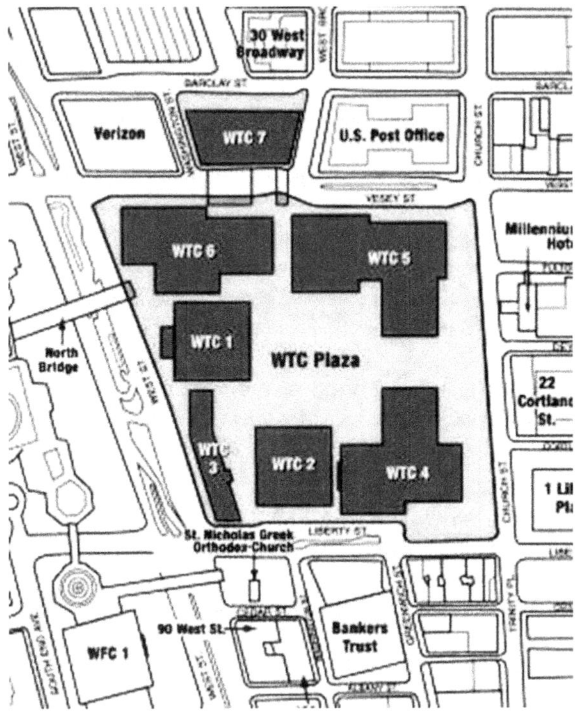

WTC-2 falls at 9.59am, WTC-1 at 10.28am.

The third tower, WTC-7, 49 story building, is intentionally demolished by the fireman at 5.20pm.

It had not been hit by an airplane, nor damaged by the ruins. It was on fire and, since it was not possible to extinguish the fire, they chose to demolish it. (?!)

It happens that the building housed the offices of the CIA, the FBI, IRS and the *"U.S.: Securities and Exchange Commission"* and they lost all the data of their work.

Tenant	Square Feet	Floor	Industry
Salomon Smith Barney	1,202,900	GRND,1-6,13,18-46	Financial Institution
IRS Regional Council	90,430	24, 25	Government
U.S. Secret Service	85,343	9,10	Government
C.I.A.	N/A	N/A	Government
American Express Bank International	106,117	7,8,13	Financial Institution
Standard Chartered Bank	111,398	10,13,26,27	Financial Institution
Provident Financial Management	9,000	7,13	Financial Institution
ITT Hartford Insurance Group	122,590	19-21	[Insurance]
First State Management Group, Inc	4,000	21	Insurance
Federal Home Loan Bank	47,490	22	Financial Institution
NAIC Securities	22,500	19	Insurance
Securities & Exchange Commission	106,117	11,12,13	Government
Mayor's Office of Emergency Mgmt	45,815	23	Government

This list is based on a table published by CNN.com. As you might have noticed, the lease of the CIA bureau is missing and was published from *New York Times del 4/11/2001 (James Risen)* only after the attack.

Another strange and uncommon fact of that dayis the rate of collapse of the towers, close to that of the force of gravity; in other words, the entire structure has almost not encountered resistance.

Physics does not even explain how a 104 story steel building can collapse without doing any resistance and keeping its axis.

Moreover there is a physics problem: steel does not allow the fall rate of a structure to be faster than usual, as it has been found, quite the opposite.

3 conditions occur to have such an event:

The breaking strength points positioned in each floor do not actually operate properly .

The breaking strength is lacking at the single floors.

Thevariance of 1/10 of a second from floor to floor.

The fragments of steel structures would be essential in the inspection, , but the inquiring committee discovered that since September 29 all pieces had been removed, due to orders of the Federal Emergency Management Agency (FEMA) and only 150 pieces (on hundreds of thousands) were "chosen" by FEMA as evidence .

Always according to FEMA, more than 350,000 tons of steel were extracted from *Ground-Zero* and "promptly" transferred to 4 firms that reused the steel:

1. Hugo Nue Schnitzer in Fresh Kills dump, Staten Island, NJ

2. Hugo Nue Schnitzer Claremont (CM) Terminal in Jersey City,

3. Metal management in Newark (NW), NJ

4. Blanford e Co. in Keasbey (KB), NJ

Assuming that the people in charge of FEMA considered the steel structures as mere debris and useless to any investigation, they certainly took care to place them nowhere else than in the decided melting furnaces.

In fact, GPS tracking devices were installed on each of the trucks that hauled away the steel from Ground-Zero, at a cost of $ 1,000 each.

(The website securitysolutions.com has an article on how to track this signal).

Moreover, the "Building Performance Assessment Team" (FEMA's BPAT), who later wrote the " WTC Buildings performance study," were not given access to Ground-Zero and were not even allowed to collect any sample of the steel found nearby, as shown in Appendix D of the same study.

Larry Silverstein, the holder of the leasing concerning the three buildings, admitted that he received a phone call from firemen who invited him to dispose of the demolition of the 3rd palace because of the huge fire.

In less than two hours from the decision , the structure of the entire building of 49 floors was studied in detail, its points of failure were located and the place to put the explosive (well over 49 floors!) was chosen. Clearly everything perfectly fit to ensure a harmless explosion for the neighbourhood.

Whilst they had been analysing these details, the explosives necessary to demolish a 49 story building was delivered, and the demolition was perfect !

I repeat: all this happened in less than two hours, whilst the whole area had been devastated from the collapse of the two towers.

Really, congratulations!

I wonder how multinationals' experts in the area can take so many weeks to prepare demolitions .

This is how the tower WTC-7 disappeared "because of a fire".

 ?!

On 9 February 2009, in Beijing, a 44-story skyscraper burns completely, until the fire extinguishes, without crashing.

In the history concerning buildings, it never happened that a steel building collapsed.

Never. No exceptions made!!!

It simply ceases to burn when the inflammable material ends.

Moreover, buildings without steel composition have structural failures firstly in a area and this fact causes then the direction of the crash . They do not crash floor by floor, perfectly standing on their axis.

Sooner or later, when it is falling, the building will encounter a structural friction that changes the way it is falling, especially if there is a steel frame to hold the building.

Who can tell what really happened on September 11?

The point is that, whatever happened really, it has currently changed the course of history - and not just because of the massacre, but even because of the phantasmagoric media event that has been expertly assembled.

For example, we are prone to be suspicious of a community , that could be just part of a system ... Without realizing it.

We experience the "institutionalized paranoia" about the surveillance in the airports. You must throw away the nail file and then on board dinner is served with metal cutlery.

We get x rayed, even our shoes and cannot bring liquids more than 100cc in cabin.

On the other hand you can carry an atomic bomb on a train or a ship carrying up to 10 times the number of passengers and maybe you can even get help from a porter.

It all seems a bit funny, don't you agree?

But even this does not happen "by accident" ... and soon we'll find out.

Social Hypnosis

Each one of us lives in three worlds...

The first world gathers the things that are <u>not</u> under our control, that we cannot change. For example:

<u>The Climate</u>:

Nothing we can do about it. If it is going to rain, it will rain.

<u>The Politics</u>:

 If you are not an activist, your vote counts 1 over 35 million.

<u>Sports</u>:

if you are not a professional player, you can only cheer on your team although you think your scarf or hat can bring good luck.

<u>News</u>:

You only know what is happening if you are the thief or the one kidnapped.

<u>Gossip</u>:

Same as above, if you are not the person of interest you will not know much.

<u>Natural disasters</u>:

No one can determine when or whether the tsunami is going to hit.

<u>Catastrophes:</u>

The bridge will fall when it will fall.

The second world gathers the things that are not under our control, but we can merely "influence".

Why do I think in the second world we have very little chance to influence?

Because our experience tells us that we cannot change our closest people's attitude except they agree. Isn't it?

Assuming that *"if you sleep with dogs you will wake up with fleas"* - that is to say we can "influence" each other when we live closely - we could acknowledge we leave our mark but do not rely on this because it could be frustrating.

The third world gathers things we can completely control and influence.

In this world we are "ourselves"!

Whatever we decide, it happens . Whether it is stop smoking, rather than starting to smoke ... Learning a new language ... Losing weight rather than gaining weight ... To enrol in a gym ...

Whatever we choose to do, it happens because in this world we "take the control" and, therefore, "influence".

Yet have you ever realised what do the media direct our "attention" to?!

Let's see together! Linger on each item7topic: Climate! Politics! Sports! News! Gossip! Cataclysms! Misfortunes!

The media engage us in the macrocosm of everything that we cannot take control of and that we cannot influence. They want us to be "distracted" and "standard", congruent with the model they like as we have seen at the beginning with the Avian flu facts, the Scazzi case, the Schettino affair...

The media make a "herd" of us, so that they can decide when it is time to return to the fold or be sheared!

One thing is certain, though: the media want to keep us away from anything that can distract us and solicit our curiosity.

They want us standard !

Also the educational system is keeping us away from what we could really learn to become "someone who thinks".

Schools do not teach communication, self esteem, leadership, the monetary system, healthy diet...but they fail you if you do not know when Garibaldi was born, or where did Napoleon die, who did what...

The history they teach us is the perfect one for the public opinion, not the real one.

Do you remember?

"We will have a worldwide control, like it or not. The only question is if this control will result from the citizens' approval or the conquest".

Nowadays

On December 23, 1913, not only was the birth of the FED, but <u>the foundations of the entire western banking system were laid</u> .

The FED gave birth to the BCE. The BCE is absorbing the entire European banking system.

Each firm is interconnected with the other one. Each one owns shares of the other firms and everything is so well entangled that you cannot see the starting point.

This situation has been ingeniously devised , and it is now impossible to right the wrongs!

But the question is, who is controlling and directing all that ?

Good question indeed! It is time to "capitalise" on everything that we have talked so far.

Let's begin: everything started from the FED!

The Fed is a "private" company that belongs to a half dozen people we already know by now and many of which, if you remember, come from "Frankfurt-am-Main" and are then interconnected to the same family, but let's see who are the shareholders of the FED:

- <u>Rothschild</u> Bank of London

- <u>Kuhn & Loeb</u> Bank of New York

- <u>Warburg</u> Bank of Hamburg

- Israel Moses Seif Banks of Italy *(heirs Rothschild)*

- Goldman-Sachs N.Y.

- <u>Warburg</u> Bank Amsterdam

- Lazard Brothers Paris

Chase Manhattan Bank NY (<u>Rockefeller</u>)

And surprise, surprise....!

Here they are, the same people and few other companies, but if we look into these latters we will find: J.P. Morgan, Warburg, Rockefeller and last but not least, Rothschild.

The banks that are part of the FED control - by a sharing system - all the Central Banks of the European Union, each one of them, the Swiss banks included!

Some examples: Goldman-Sachs is one of the biggest shareholders of Unicredit, but Unicredit is a shareholder of Bankitalia that owns 15% of the BCE.

J.P. Morgan is one of the biggest shareholders of M.P.S.

Barclays is one of the biggest shareholders of Intesa-San Paolo, that is, too, a shareholder of Bankitalia...

All this situation has been accurately created and there is <u>no coming back</u>!

It is the whole system that has to be taken down.

The following is a typical example of "media" and "hypnotic" communication:

The BCE has as its most important shareholders: Germany (23,4%), France (16,5%), England (16%), Italy (14,5%) and others...

I spoke about *"countries"* and for this reason you could think of the governments... but it is not exact! They are actually <u>private</u> institutes!

I wonder why England refuses to join the common currency and is financially involved, isn't it ?

The truth is the "government" is not involved, but the private institutes headed by the well kwon family are! .

By the way, the 23,4% of shares owned by Germany in the BCE is the reason why this country has a lot of power of decision in the European union.

Let's now see the main shareholders of Bankitalia:

- Intesa-San Paolo (united with Barclays) 45%

-    Unicredit-Capitalia
(Goldman Sachs, JP Morgan) 22%

You should know that many of the trust companies behind these "international" institutions have registered offices at the Cayman Islands.

 ?!

Let's now find out well known people who had connection with Goldman Sachs together with relevant offices in Europe:

Mario Draghi

Governor of the Banca d'Italia from 2006 to 2011 and Governor of the BCE since 2011. He was vice-president of Goldman Sachs for Europe from 2002 to 2005.

Gianni Letta

State Undersecretary at the Presidency of the Ministries Council during Silvio Berlusconi era . He has been appointed advisor of Goldman Sachs in 2007.

Mario Monti

European Commissioner from 1994 to 2004. Prime Minister of Italy since 2011. He has been an advisor at Goldman Sachs.

Lucas Papademos

Prime Minister of Greece since 2011. From 1994 to 2002 has been Governor of the Greek Central Bank

Some other people who came in contact with Goldman Sachs and had relevant governmental jobs

Mark Carney

Governor of the Bank of Canada since 2008 and Chairman of the Financial Stability Board since 2001, he worked for thirteen years at Goldman Sachs.

Romano Prodi

President of IRI from 1982 to 1989 and from 1993 to 1994, Prime Minister of Italy from 1996 to 1998 and from 2006 to 2008.

Also President of the European Commission from 1999 to 2004, he was a consultant at Goldman Sachs from 1990 to 1993 and after 1997.

Massimo Tononi

Economy Undersecretary of the second Prodi government from 2006 to 2008 and President of the Italian Stock Exchange since 2011, he was a partner and advisory director at Goldman Sachs.

François Hollande seems to appear "all of a sudden" and is voted President of France. But after just two months he gives the BCE the power to control the French banks.

A few months ago "il Giornale", a local newspaper, stated the following:

"Another Goldman-Sachs in command of Europe: Mark Carney, already Governor of the Central Bank of Canada, is elected Governor of the Bank of England!".

What about the "IMF"?

The International Monetary Fund (IMF) and the World Bank (BM), were conceived during the well-known *"Bretton Woods Conference"* in New New Hampshire, 1944.

At the end of the meeting , Nixon announced to the country and to the entire world that the relationship between the dollar and the gold stock would cease to exist, and there would be a 10% more of taxes on importations...

(If you are curious, try looking up information of that specific conference. It has many different possible interpretations).

The United States of America, that draw up the original document of the IMF and participate with 18% to the vote, decided that important decisions could be validatedwith 85% of the Board of Administration ayes.

Insiders know that the IMF is run by Washington. It is no coincidence that its office is there.

The members of the IMF are the representatives of the most influential countries, first of all the United States.

Both the IMF and the World Bank were established with the "official" purpose of: *stabilise exchange rates and, as soon as World War 2 ended, help the reconstruction of the international world by facilitating countries in difficulty in the payment of their debts.*

Apparently it seems a remarkable aim . Here's how it works:

The members deposit money through a quota system, creating resources for the operations of the IMF in favour of countries with financial difficulties which can draw on loans.

Through these activities and others, such as the surveillance of the economies of its members and policies, the IMF works to improve the economies of its member countries.

Wow! Don't you want to contribute to this "humanitarian crusade"?!

But let's see what happens most of the time ...

When the IMF intervenes in favour of a country in difficulty asking for emergency loans to pay off a debt or to overcome a currency crisis, the approach that the IMF adopts seems to be more or less standard, whether the counterpart is Russia, Argentina, Zimbabwe or South Korea, even though the cultures, economies and situations are very different.

IMF is willing to help a state in need as long as the state uses the supervision of multinationals with experience in the area and connected to the IMF !

Often the IMF calls this agreement *"The Washington Consensus"*, a fancy name given in 1990 by the American economist and supporter of the IMF, John Williamson, to describe the way the IMF works.

Not only this term supports the theory that the IMF is controlled by Washington, but it also gives a kind of "sovereignty" to the Fund's activity.

Most of the time the IMF helps the state in need and asks the privatisation of state-owned industries, the public spending review and cuts, both in the educational and health area, the devaluation of the national currency against the dollar and the introduction the *'free flow of international assets".* in this way the circulation of assets coming from the multinationals connected to IMF are favoured.

Given that the IMF represents enormous private assets and banks, its role goes far beyond , whether it is the World Bank or private banks, investors etc..

As the investors want to gain from the financial transactions, the <u>local currency has to be devalued against the dollar</u>.

Usually the local politicians take part to the lucrative and "advantageous" business of the privatisation process. In this way the multinationals acquire mines, petrol, pipelines, water and other national treasures in perfect conditions.

The Yeltsin government has been a typical scenario of this. In Russia, the Yeltsin government allowed resourceful businessman to quickly become billionaires, buying the national goods with the help and support of the IMF that asked for the privatisations.

The Clinton administration, always through the IMF, supported this plan, sure that it would transform Russia into an further dollar area.

To understand the extent of the "multinationals" power and, therefore, the situations out of balance that this supremacy generates , just think of Tanzania GDP (total turnover of a country): $ 2.2 billion with a population of around 25 million people, while for example, Goldman Sachs profits are $ 2.5 billion with 160 shareholders .

(Dr. Susan George "Fate worse than debt")

But we will return to the real hidden power of the multinationals .

Who's behind all this?

The game is extremely intriguing if you try to figure it out, because more and more various secret companies *(always less secret)* lay behind the "big plan" (even if they are managed quite always by the same people or by new ones here or there, according to the objective of the single company).

Daniel Estulin has investigated and researched for over a decade, the Bilderberg Group and his "profound impact" on the economy, finance, global politics, war, peace, and control the world's resources and its money.

Daniel is still considered among the most knowledgeable on the subject and is often invited to speak on television and on the news.

His book, "The Bilderberg Club," was published in 2005 and has been updated to a new edition in 2009.

On May 29, 1954 at the "Hotel de Bilderberg" in Oosterbeek, Holland, the most powerful men in the world arranged a meeting for the first time, to discuss the future of the world and decided to schedule it every year and keep it secret.

The group took its name from the hotel where they met: *"Bilderberg Group"*.

The members of the group represent the elite of the dominance in the world and are mostly from America, Canada and Western Europe with familiar names like *David Rockefeller, Henry Kissinger, Bill Clinton, Gordon Brown, Angela Merkel, Alan Greenspan, Ben Bernanke, Larry Summers, Tim Geithner, Lloyd Blankfein, George Soros, Donald Rumsfeld, Rupert Murdoch* and then heads of state, influential senators, congressmen and parliamentarians, Pentagon and NATO members, members of European royalty, selected media figures, the most influential people of the *"Council on Foreign Relations"* (CFR), IMF, World Bank, the *Trilateral Commission*, EU, and powerful central bankers of the Federal Reserve, the BCE, and the *Bank of England.*

In its early days, the Bilderberg Group had objective to: *"Create an aristocracy of intentions between Europe and the United States in order to rule the world in the field of politics, economy, resources and the overall strategy."*

NATO has played an essential role guaranteeing a state of "endless war", no matter where...

The Group is made up of members *(approximately one hundred of the most influential people in the world)* that reunite once a year, sometimes with other members too chosen for their expertise and influence in specific areas, sometimes with rookies that could result useful contacts in the future.

Those with high potential are invited to come back.

In his book, Estulin shows that the former Arkansas governor, Bill Clinton, attended the Bilderberg meeting in 1991 and on that occasion David Rockefeller explained that the North American Free Trade Agreement *("North American Free Trade Agreement" : NAFTA)* was a priority for the Bilderberg Group and asked him to help them realize it .

"By an odd twist of fate" Clinton was elected president the following year and on January 1, 1994, the NAFTA program e came into effect.

The key they use is to choose preselected people to put as head of the country, the army and other crucial positions...

(If these facts are of interest for you read more in his book)

This is not the "only" group existing...

In May 1919, at the Hotel Majestic in Paris, it was held a reunion between British and Americans, for the "Peace Conference"...

Following his meeting the *"Royal Institute of International Affairs"* (RIIA) and of the *"Council on Foreign Relations"* were founded.

The Council on Foreign Relations (CFR) is a private American organisation, with no political interests. Among its members are government officials, business executives, journalists, educators and students, civic and religious leaders, and other interested citizens that debate on world problems and foreign policy choices facing the United States and other countries.

Founded in 1921, its headquarters are located in New York and Washington.

One of its founding members was Edward Mandell House - Head Counsellor of President Woodrow Wilson - who signed the constitution act of the Federal Reserve and the following February validated *"the 16th amendment"* (he gave birth to the *"federal income tax"* that allowed the country to pay its "public debt" thanks to the incoming).

Since its establishment, the CFR promotes globalization based on a centralized funding system

Today, CFR has thousands of influential members, with a key role in the major media, but keeps a low public profile, especially regarding the actual agenda.

The historian Arthur Schlesinger, Jr. has called CFR :

"A front organization for the heart of the American Establishment" whose members arranges private meetings and tell people only what they like to say. "

Its members are all Americans.

To have an idea of how "strong" this private organization just look at its past and present members :

Nearly all candidates for the presidency (of both parties, as you can never be too cautious...)

The most influent senators and members of the Congress...

The key members of the media world and their chiefs...

FBI, CIA, NSA officials and also other members of important governmental firms.

The CFR has been a virtual employment agency for both Democrats' and Republicans' employees.

Regardless of who has been in command of the White House, the power of the CFR and its "agenda" have remained unchanged since it was founded in 1921.

The CFR calls for the establishment of a "global super-state", in which America and other nations sacrifice their sovereignty in favour of a central power.

 ?!

Remember the famous words pronounced by Warburg at the Senate of the United States:

"We will have a worldwide control, like it or not. The only question is if this control will result from the citizens' approval or the conquest".

Years later, during a meeting with the Bilderberg Group in 1992, Henry Kissinger stated:

"Today, Americans would be outraged if UN troops entered Los Angeles to restore order; tomorrow, they will be grateful. This is especially true if they were told there was an outside threat from beyond, whether real or promulgated, that threatened our very existence. It is then that all people of the world will plead with world leaders to deliver them from this evil....individual rights will be willingly relinquished for the guarantee of their well-being granted to them by their world government."

This conception, that has its roots in the "Hegelian Dialectics" and is recurring today, consists in 3 stages:

Create a problem.

Check the reaction.

Offer a solution.

Pay close attention: everything told since this point has the same dynamic, starting with the founding of the FED.

The CFR was formed to create a "New World Order" (get used with this term and you will understand later) and the "United Nations" had been founded by a some CFR members called "the Informal Agenda Group ".

These people composed the original draft of the UN organization and , presented it to Franklin Roosevelt who announced it publically the following day.

At the moment of its founding, in 1945, the CFR was composed of more than 40 delegates from the United States.

According to Professor William G. Domhoff, author of "Who Rules America", the CFR operates through small groups or companies of about twenty five people. It brought together the major world leaders of 9 categories (industrialists, financiers, ideologues, military, specific professionals, lawyers, doctors, and workers' organisations, trade unions) for detailed discussions on specific topics in the field of foreign policy.

Domhoff added:

"The CFR, while not financed by the government, works closely with it, so it is difficult to think that the action of the CFR is stimulated independently of the government, when its main actions end up financing the most important foundations such as the Rockefeller, Carnegie, and Ford (to name just three) and they are all run by major corporate officers of the CFR itself. "

Source

"The True Story of the Bilderberg Group" and What They May Be Planning Now | Global Research. 2012. "The True Story of the Bilderberg Group" and What They May Be Planning Now | Global Research. [Accessed 29 December 2012].

Organisations and institutions, never people!

Daniel Estulin not only describes, but "documents" also, in his book, the involvement of Henry Kissinger and the Bildenberg Group behind the murder of Aldo Moro.

"In 1982, John Coleman, a former intelligence agent who was able to access all stages of power and all the secret papers, revealed that the former Italian Prime Minister Aldo Moro, a senior member of the Christian Democrats, who was opposing the "zero growth" and the policies of population reduction planned for his country, was killed by the P2 Masonic lodge, in order to bend Italy to the wishes of the "Club of Rome" and the Bilderberg group, both aimed at de-industrialise the country and reduce significantly the population. "

In "The Conspirators Circle 1," Coleman says that the forces of the globalisation wanted to use Italy to destabilise the Middle East, their real target.

"Moro planned to stabilize Italy through full employment and industrial and political peace, strengthening the Catholic opposition to communism and making

the destabilization of the Middle East more difficult to obtain."

Coleman describes in detail the sequence of events that paralyzed Italy: the kidnapping in broad daylight of Aldo Moro by the Red Brigades; the merciless execution of his escort and his murder.

On November 10, 1982 , Corrado Guerzoni, a close friend of the victim, giving his testimony at the Court in Rome said : "Aldo Moro was threatened by an officer of the" Royal Institute for International Affairs "(RIIA), while he was still minister ".

Coleman said that during the trial of the members of the Red Brigades, many of them testified that a high official of the United States was involved in the murder of Moro.

Moreover, between June and July 1982, the widow of Aldo Moro testified that the murder of her husband had been the result of a series of threats to his life, moved by someone, that she described as: "A very important figure of the American politics."

When the judge asked her if she could refer to the Court what he said, Eleonora Moro repeated exactly the things that Guerzoni had previously expressed: "If you do not change your policy , you will pay your obstinacy! ".

Coleman adds: "When Guerzoni , was asked by the judge if he was able to identify the person described by Mrs. Moro, he answered that she was talking about Henry Kissinger", as he had already stated previously.

The question now might be: Why would an important American politician threaten a leader of an independent European nation?

On November 10, 1982, the "stunning" testimony of Guerzoni, potentially dangerous for the relationship between United States and Italy, spread out in all Western European media. Oddly enough, , , no American tv channel gave prominence to this news, even though <u>Kissinger had been indicted for complicity in the murder</u>!

But this silence is not so surprising, as we will understand better later on, when we speak about the "Council on Foreign Relations" (CFR).

Note that it was Aldo Moro that wanted the emission of money without debt, therefore without interests for approximately 500 billion lire during the 60s and 70s, with the 500 lire banknote that displayed "legal tender". *

Prime 500 lire cartacee biglietto di Stato serie "Aretusa"

Seconda serie: "Mercurio"

This note had the purpose to input money without creating debts, to help the Italian government pay off the interests originating by the central banking system.

" It happened ", one more time, that Aldo Moro was murdered!

89

Carlos Calçada Bastos

*   *The 500 lire were emitted from "Aretusa" e "Mercurio".*

The first emission was placed under the DPR 20-06-1966 and 20-10-1967 from President Giuseppe Saragat for the 500 lire banknote by Aretusa, (Law 31-05-1966).

The second emission was controlled with DPR 14-02-1974, from President Giovanni Leone (for the 500 lire banknote by Mercurio, DM 2 april 1979)

C.F.R. - R.I.I.A., nothing else?

Let us speak now of the "Trilateral Commission", founded in June 23, 1973, commissioned by David Rockefeller who is also a leading member of the Bilderberg Group, and Honorary Chairman of the CFR.

The Trilateral Commission is similar to the CFR, a non-governmental, non-partisan discussion group to foster closer cooperation among North America, Western Europe, and .

Thanks to the Trilateral Commission the term "technocracy" has been forged to define a political philosophy whose tactics pivot on two main facts:

The inter-dependence of people entangled in a web of relationships.

A system of society beyond the concept of "national sovereignty".

Recently, for the first time in history, two states had a "technical government" and have been - coincidentally - both ruled by members of the Trilateral Commission: Greece with Papademos (Vice President ECB) and Italy with Mario Monti, who in 2010 was even President for Europe of the Trilateral!

Zbigniew Brzezinski - founding member of the Trilateral Commission - issued a report on "St. Petersburg Times "August 2, 1974 entitled " The crisis of democracy ".

According to Brzezinski, in the United States the efficiency of the White House was vitiated by an excess of democracy and , since the 60s, the governments of Eastern Europe were literally overwhelmed by the excessive participation of people, and by requests that the bureaucracies were not able to dispose of, so that political systems were ungovernable. Also, the only democracies that have ever worked were those where a significant part of the population has remained on the margins of political debate, literally " breath holding ".

In fact, the Trilateral took control of the executive in America and influenced it over the last thirty years.

Still now the idea that the States – as we think of them in a standard way - are no longer essential for the community and may be replaced with a unique government that supervises the entire world, prevails.

As you may be skeptical about this vision, I invite you to check it out before you discard it, since several presidents have tried to make it public domain – even if they did not succeed - some of them at the cost of their life.

For example, Ronald Reagan, in the pre-election period went on promising that if elected, he would investigate the Trilateral Commission, and would never allow George Bush (father) to have a place in his administration - arguing that Bush was a member of both the Trilateral and the CFR. Regan, as you know, wiped out the act of JF Kennedy 11,110,

Yet, when elected, Reagan nominated George Bush Vice President!... ...

Wow! What a turnaround.

If you think that George Bush (the father) was not only a member of the Trilateral, but also a member of the CFR and member of "Skull and Bones" (one of the best known and most discussed secret societies in the United States and whose headquarter is in the prestigious Yale University) it is easy "to understand " what happened ...

The above mentioned societies perfectly succeed in their objectives, given any kind of obstacle, and this is why Regan chose George Bush as the man in the command of the United States after him.

Another president who spoke explicitly to the nation about these secret societies and their purpose was JF Kennedy.

Below is the transcript of one of his "last" speeches to the nation, before being murdered. Although it will take no more than five minutes to read it, at least read the underlined parts:

"The word "secret" is horrible in a free and open society and we are a population intrinsically and historically against the "secret societies", to the "secret oaths" and to the "secret procedures"...

A long time ago we decided that the dangers of the excessive concealing and, most importantly, not justified, of facts can go far more beyond the dangers of absolving.

There is not much to do, nowadays, to oppose these menaces of a closed society.

There is not much sense in wanting to ensure the survival of our nation if our traditions do not survive with it.

There is a serious danger, that promises to dramatically increase the pressure for safety, placed in the hands of those who are eager to expand it up to the limits of official censorship and concealment.

I do not mean to allow it, as long as it is not under my control and no member of my administration, regardless of whether they are high or low rank, whether civilian or military, should interpret my words tonight as an excuse to censor the news, to stifle dissent, to cover up our mistakes or to deny to the press and the public the facts they deserve to know.

<u>We are opposed to a monolithic and ruthless conspiracy that relies on secret means for expanding its sphere of influence, the "infiltration" instead of invasion, on "subversion" instead of elections, "intimidation" instead of free choice , on the "guerrillas by night" instead of armies by day.</u>

<u>It is a system that involves a large number of human and material resources in order to build a thick knit, highly efficient machine that involves militaries,</u>

diplomats, "intelligence" operations economic, scientific and political.

Their creations are hidden, non-public information. Their mistakes are buried not in evidence. Their dissenters are silenced, not praised. No expenditure is questioned, no rumor is printed, no secret is revealed.

No president should fear the "public" poll of his program because it is from that scrutiny that comes understanding, and from understanding comes support or opposition. Both are necessary.

I am not asking your newspapers to support the Administration, but I ask your help in the tremendous task of informing and alerting the American people.

I have full confidence in the response and dedication of our citizens ... Whenever you are fully informed.

I not only do not stifle controversy among the readers, but I welcome that. This Administration intends to be honest about his mistakes, because as a wise man once said: "An error does not become a mistake until you refuse to correct the problem."

We intend to accept full responsibility for our mistakes, and we expect that there will facades notes.

Without debate, without criticism, no administration and no country can succeed - and no republic can survive. That is why the Athenian lawmaker Solon ruled a crime to any citizen who abstained from debate.

This is why our press was protected by the First Amendment right: The only business in America specifically protected by the Constitution, not primarily to amuse and entertain, not to emphasise the trivial and the sentimental, not even to give the public what it wants but to inform, to arouse, to reflect, to state our dangers and our opportunities, to indicate our crises and our choices, to lead, educate and sometimes even the anger of the public opinion itself.

This means better information and analysis of international news, because overseas is no longer far away, but close at hand and local.

This means greater attention to improved understanding of the news, improved communication, and finally, it means that governments at all levels, must meet its obligation to provide the most complete information possible in accordance *with the narrowest limits of national security.*

<u>And so it is for the press, responsible for documenting the actions of man, the keeper of his conscience, the courier of his news, that we look for strength and support, confident that with your help man will be what he was born to be: free and independent. "</u>

He was murdered a few months later!

And the original picture

continues

George W. Bush took over the project that Bill Clinton began with the *"North American Free Trade Agreement"* (NAFTA, remember?).

His commitment to the further development of the union between Mexico, Canada and the United States was admirable.

I know it may sound fine , it recalls popular values and concepts: Union... Development... Mutual support... etc. but let's see what happened and what is happening, from the "back door"...

On March 23, 2005, the leaders of Canada, Mexico and the United States (George W. Bush) met at "Baylor University", in Waco (Texas), and on the pressing questions of the purpose of the meeting it was only told that it was simple "handshake" ...

Unfortunately, a few weeks later, it was found out that there had been another "secret" meeting. The three governments refused to give any information regarding it and simply told it was a meeting for reasons of state. (?!)

From 12 to 14 September 2006 a few dozens of representatives of the three governments met secretly at the *Fairmont Banff Springs Hotel"* of Banff (Canada).

A year later, when the media uncovered that meeting and asked for the agenda of it, they were diverted for "national security" reasons. (?!)

You see, in a society characterized by "media-hypnosis of the mass" like ours, moving is easier for those who have control of the game, since the citizens are focused on more important issues as: Climate! Politics! News! Gossip! Disasters!

Does it ring a bell?! 

In this way, under the facade of social commitment, mutual collaboration between countries and everything that the people likes to chat about, Bush takes over what his predecessor Bill Clinton began with "NAFTA". This time Bush extends its operation to the economics sectors as for example, energy, communication, military, financial, banking!!!

This new project was publicly defined as: *"Security and Prosperity Partnership of North America"* (SPP) with the aim to copy the European community: the union of the states

The SPP has thus laid the foundation for "collaboration" (what else ever?) between the United States and Mexico and Canada ... Yeah!

But now we have to reflect on which kind of cooperation may be between the gigantic United States and the two neighbours ...

No wonder if the secret project is to introduce a single currency for all the three states as it happened in Europe with the Euro.

Sounds good, right?

There are rumours that say that the FED has already tested the new currency and that it will be named *"Amero"*.

Try surfing on the web...

FEDERAL RESERVE NOTE SPECIMENS
INAUGURATION · 2010 SERIES · INITIAL PRINTING
UNION OF NORTH AMERICA
1
5
5
10
10
10
10
20
20
20
20
50
FIFTY
50
50
100
100
100
200
200
200
PRETRIAL SPECIMENS ONLY · NOT AUTHORIZED FOR CIRCULATION OR PUBLIC RELEASE

The question now is:

"To realise such a project a Central Bank like the one existing in Europe is required , isn't it?"

Yes... it is!

Which one of the banks do we refer to?

The Mexican?

Or maybe the Canadian one?

Or "maybe"... the FED?!

Who knows?!

Let's wait and see.

Conclusions?

I think it is naive to make "conclusions" on a picture that exists since the existence of the so called "Illuminati" and whose tactics are constantly modified to satisfy their needs. Their aim is the "total globalisation" or, as the various leaders like to call it, the "New Worldwide Order".

Seriously?

Another philosophical conspiracy?! Drawn by Carlos, all philosophical and optimist...

I think this is not a "conspiracy", but a simple picture originated centuries ago, wisely and well pursued with extreme excellence.

That's it. Regardless of its purpose, I admit to being totally enraptured by the demonstrated mastery over the centuries and carefully passed down from generation to generation ...

If the people were not in a "self-social-hypnosis" status and used the Internet differently, they might realise the frequent use in the history of the term "New World Order" and the circumstance that these words always come from the same powerful people.

In a context of international relations, the phrase "New World Order" is often used as a reference to a "new period" ... as a result of dramatic events.

(Sounds familiar?)

In the 20th and 21st century many statesman used these words, such as Woodrow Wilson, Winston Churchill, Michail Gorbačëv, Gerald Ford, George H.W. Bush, Henry Kissinger, Gordon Brown, referring to a *"new history era"*, as it happened after World War 2 or the Cold War...

I do not think that it can be called a "coincidence" that the back of the dollar note had the Masonry symbol since 1935.

Even Obama frequently uses this idea of "new worldwide order".

Talking of Obama..

These are the pictures of an article from *"NewsWeek" (2008)* in which Evan Thomas remembered the new President of the United States that he is "super partes" and it is expected not to show emblems resembling his convictions ... or the origins of his convictions!

Let's watch it more closely..

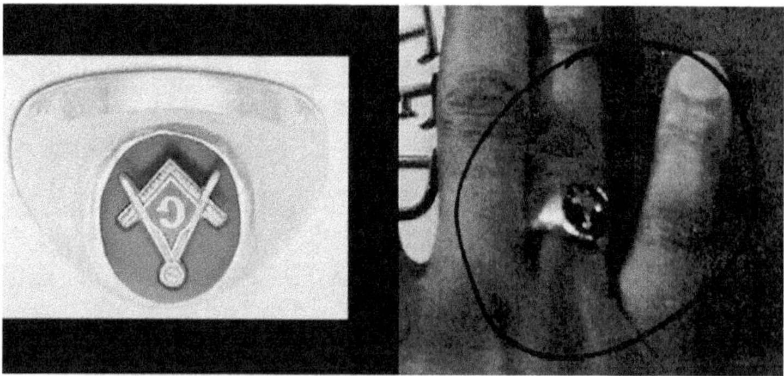

As if it was not enough, to understand the origins of that ring and of the symbol...

So there are no "conclusions" to propose , if anything, raise the threshold of attention when we hear things regarding the Fed, the ECB, RIIA (Royal Institute of International Affairs), CFR (Council on Foreign Relations), the IMF (International Monetary Fund), WB (World Bank) or the Trilateral Commission ...

Now we know that all these "Official Institutions" are nothing more than PRIVATE structures, and as such, it is wise to think that they will follow their "private" interests!

For example, we should reflect the reason why the IMF has

openly opposed the abolition of tax IMU in Italy, which "coincidentally" has been proposed by the Monti government .. But, if we want to give the IMF an institutional role (although it is a private institution), it would conform to the economical aspect of the country, wouldn't it?!

As to speak of "Official Institutions" .. even the famous three "Rating" agencies such as Fitch, Standard & Poor's and Moody's are PRIVATE companies. They do not acquaint us with the method of analysis they use to come to "their" assessments; their procedure has never been made public, but those valuations are guidelines for investors of all over the world!

Surely their "rating" on the company's activities often results in a large inflow of capital from investors, rather than an equally massive outflow of capital.

The same applies when the states are subject to evaluation.

Moreover, the valuations they do often reveal wrong and we should make a reflection on it : for example Irelandhas been rated AAA (triple A) even after its financial problems were made public. Spain has also had AAA rating until 2009, shortly before the collapse. The Bond of Greece were considered "investment grade" until March 2010, just two months before the riots would start ..

What can I say?

Now that we are aware of these facts, when listening to "sensational" news by the media let us not take just note of it – like most of us do – but let ask ourselves whether it is a device to push us later on into decisions that advantage "other" interests, (let us not forget the well known Hegelian Dialectics).

Now we can properly " understand" what goes unnoticed to the crowd, such as realizing that it was the current Greek Prime Minister, put in charge to "save" Greece, to bring the country into the euro system ... delivering it to the arms of ECB!

The Italian politicians who, casually, are named in "these pages" brought us in the Euro zone ..

So, whatever happens, do not worry. The technic is to "engulf" and then whatever pantomimic is set up, no one will ever be excluded .. "Whatever the cost"!

Have you still doubts?

David Rockefeller in his book "Memoirs" of 2002 on page 405, quotes:

For more than a century ideological extremists at either end of the political spectrum have seized upon well-publicized incidents such as my encounter with Castro to attack the Rockefeller family for the inordinate influence they claim we wield over American political and economic institutions. Some even believe we are part of a secret cabal working against the best interests of the United States, characterizing my family and me as 'internationalists' and of conspiring with others around the world to build a more integrated global political and economic structure -- one world, if you will. If that's the charge, I stand guilty, and I am proud of it."

You know what I think?

I think that in this plan the "internet" is (at least now) just a "pebble in the shoe" and I would not be surprised if soon something "sensational" hits the world, so that a severe intervention and control is required , obviously, as always, in the name of "public good!

Just recently (early February 2013), the Pentagon has publicly announced that they are taking 4,000 hackers to "protect" themselves against the risk of attacks ...

This news was given by all the media, and they made you perceive the fact as a "necessity" (Hegelian dialectics, remember?) People in self-hypnosis cannot notice "nuts and bolts" .

I think it's pretty naive to manage the assumption of "FOUR THOUSAND" people (please reflect on the number) to develop a protection program. (?)

Think of hiring 100 people for a "project". It is a considerable number of people even for a big company.

Think of hiring 500 people. Please try to "visualize" 500 people ..

Now think of hiring ... A THOUSAND people!

Do you see the amount of human resources?!

Ok... Now think of hiring 2.000 people. Amazing, isn't it ?

2.500... !?

3.000 people for a project...!

Scary, no?!

finally skip immediately to the actual 4,000, and think of their logistics, even if they could work at home .. How many technicians do you need to "set" 4,000 employees?

Can you see clearly now the mass of this project? ...To "protect" the Pentagon from possible hacker attacks!?

Bho?!

Anyway, nobody denounced the anomalies of this project, as we use to face downwards, distracted by the news given by the media that consist in the nothing

Do you understand the reason why I suggest tospend less time watching television and more time "looking" in the network ... Believe me, you would be surprised!

Following the above mass recruitment, I assure you that in the next 2 or 3 years, as it always happened, we will experience "dangerous hacker attacks" to world security so ... The safest solution to the world is CHECK THE NETWORK!

It is the well – known scheme of the "Hegelian Dialectics" that, and after this writing I hope they will turn up to be "predictable"!

Do you remember Kissinger in 1992?

"Today, Americans would be outraged if UN troops entered Los Angeles to restore order; tomorrow, they will be grateful. This is especially true if they were told there was an outside threat from beyond, whether real or promulgated, that threatened our very existence. It is then that all people of the world will plead with world leaders to deliver them from this evil….individual rights will be willingly relinquished for the guarantee of their well-being granted to them by their world

government."

In this way the net will be a mere tool for leisure and entertainment or for gathering information on what is considered "appropriate", so as to keep the population growing in self-hypnosis and "distraction"!

History repeating itself...

History is being repeated

Now that we use "new eyes", there are so many things happened in the last two months - since I finished writing the book - .. and history seems to be repeating itself at moment with Syria and the "alleged" use of poison gas ...

The news about the deaths have been so vague, with a range between 350 and 1,500 people ... Then, some videos and photos, uploaded on the web, raise some doubts.

So far, as the media reported, there not have been serious adverse events associated with the poisonous gas for people, although the harmful effects stay on the ground for several years ... (?)

Yesterday, August 29, 2013, the British government reported that the UN Commissioners sent on-site to check the situation , have not still found evidence (?) and direct the decision to attack Syria at the UN Assembly. Russia too says that there is no evidence of the use of poisonous gas ...

Yet the United States have been promptly sending fleets to Syria and pushed its allies into attack ...

I wonder why such a punctual diligence did not show when the ex Yugoslavia had been place of internecine struggles, like a cannibal, and the media had been daily documenting the atrocity.

With the knowledge so far acquired, let us try to look at the same scenario from a different prospective

The mineral reserves of Syria are oil, natural gas, phosphates, salt and asbestos - even mined for export (in 2003 only fuels were already 71.3% of exports). In mountain regions there are also deposits of coal, iron, copper, lead and gold.

The search for sources of cheap energy is one of the geopolitical contexts that guide the war in Syria.

Christof Lehmann *(NSBC International)* wrote, in 2012:

" The discovery of the gas field in Pars, Iran, in 2007, and the plan of Tehran to build the gas pipeline for the Eastern Mediterranean through Iraq and Syria, gives Iran the chance to turn into a global economic power, and let Tehran represent a huge leverage on the EU's policy in the Middle East .

Also note that 2007 was the year in which the global economic crisis started, and again in 2007 , Saudi Arabia stated that the gas sector, no more oil is the investment of the future.

2007 was also the year in which Qatar has sent as many as 10 billion dollars for the " Freedom and Justice Party ," represented by the Prime Minister of Turkey R. Tayyip Erdogan.

The money has been given to provide the preparation of the Turkish Muslim Brotherhood for the war against Syria.

Never before the value of the Petro - Dollar has been so critical and challenged as it is today in the United States, along with the United Kingdom, that are fighting for their survival because their economies are based on the dollar. The European Union (EU) , at moment receives between 22% and 26% of its natural gas from Russia. If the Pars gas pipeline went into operation, and Russia participated in developing Syrians gas fields in the eastern Mediterranean , the EU would be dependent on Russia for 45-50 % of natural gas for the next 100-120 years.

This dependence would push many continental European countries to " integrate " further cooperation in the energy field between Europeans and Russians, but the Europeans are also aware that the U.S. evaluate the situation so risky for them to favour an adversarial relationship between Europe and Russia .

Facing this scenario, the United States have two main choices:

It could to play together with Qatar and Saudi Arabia against Syria , Iran , Russia and Western Europe or , alternatively, the United States could re-configure its national economy , and start a "dialogue ", a constructive cooperation to create a new economy based on gold and peaceful co-operation with Russia , China , Europe, and not least Iran 's energy sector .

Despite of which of these two options is going to choose the United States , the crisis in Syria threatens the global dominance of the Petro - Dollar .

The question for the U.S. is whether to risk it all, drawing the entire Middle East, Europe and Russia scenario or to retreat peacefully from the subversion of Syria and rely on Russia , China and Europe, for a new economy.

In addition, the Italian geographer Manlio Dinucci reported, contrary to the popular opinion, that Syria has huge oil and gas reserves.

Dinucci writes:

"The strategy of the U.S. / NATO, focused on supporting the rebels that occupy the oil fields, has two purpose: to deprive the state of the Syrian export earnings, already greatly diminished as a result of the EU embargo, and ensure that the great deposits could be controlled in the future by the major Western oil companies after the "rebels" occupation"

To all this must be added the statement reported by the newspapers of the U.S. Secretary of State John Kerry, that on September 7, during the meeting with the European Union's 28 Foreign Ministers, in Vilnius, said: "Obama reserves all options in the event the UN do not support the US and informs that the decision about the strategy against Damascus is independent from the report of the inspectors of the United Nations on the use of chemical weapons.

 ?!

As soon as the G20 members in St. Petersburg turn out to be in favor of a political solution, Kerry stressed the U.S. position and declared that "the military intervention in Syria could facilitate" such a possibility.

 ?!

What can I say?

Fortunately events seem to focus on a political-diplomatic strategy, but there is no doubt that the impetus and the immediacy of the response of the United States, have been at least ... "unusual"!

At this point, everyone can draw his conclusions, but at least now we have a perspective perhaps more "complete", though not necessarily the one they want you to have!

Essentially

The way of life of each of us is characterized by what we see and what we know, but we have seen previously that we are a society in which the focus is deliberately kept "somewhere else".

We're just living on the "surface" ... but on the surface of an iceberg!

"For us" the richest people in the world, amongst those that we already know, are:

Bill Gates *(US)* whose wealth is estimated at $ 74 billion.

Carlos Slim (Mexico) with 56 Billion.

Warren Buffett (United States) with 50 Billion.

Bernard Arnault (France) 41 Billion, and so on.

All the economy that we are allowed to know is represented by that point of the iceberg... But nobody asks what is underneath.

Some of us have a "vague" idea, others have resigned and others do not care and go on living ... on the surface of the iceberg!

No one has ever raised the issue that among the world's richest people the families we have talked about so far - Rockefeller, Warburg, Schiff, Rothschild, Loeb and everybody else - are not even classified...

Even through the media we never get acquainted of anything about them, their marriages, births, deaths... Nothing.

For the citizens, they do not exist, however...

There are so many sources and documentaries available, in which the assets of the Rothschilds are estimated to be between 300 and 500 ...

You should think … 300/500 "billion", shouldn't you?

Naive!

From 300 to 500 trillion. I repeat:

TRILLION!

Approximately half of the entire worlds heritage!

Do you find it "incredible"?

"Incredible" is something that we cannot give an explanation to. Think about it!

For me it is extremely "logical" that it is like this, and, maybe, it is the same for someone of you...once knowing their assets in 1818...until 1930.

You are not required to read the following, but in order to have a vague perception of "what" we are talking about, what follows is the credit situation in the world of the Rothschild family from 1818 to 1930, made public by the same family on the site:

(www.rothschildarchive.org/textguide/?doc=/textguide/articles/loans)

It is striking to look at the following list because it let us understand the entity of the financial operations they use to do and the information on the debtors: the world as a whole! Not joking!!!

The list shows that Rothschild family had been financing governments and their activities for a long time. The entire world is their debtor since a long time!

"Cash Book, Russian Loan, 1818-1819 XIII/14/1, 1 volume. A record of subscriptions for the loan. Major business of the London House, 1818-1914."

| 1818 | Prussian Government 5% Loan, £5m |
| 1819 | British Government 3% Loan, £12m |

1821	Neapolitan Government 5% Loan, 16m ducats (c.£2m) with C. M. Rothschild
1822	Prussian Government 5% Loan, £3.5m
1822	Russian Government 5% Loan, £6.6m
1822	Neapolitan Government Loan, 20m ducats (c.£2.5m), contracted for by C. M. Rothschild subscriptions received by N. M. Rothschild
1823	Portuguese Government 5% Loan at the charge of Brazilian Government, £1.5m
1823	French Government 5% Loan, f23m (c.£18.5m), contracted for by de Rothschild Frères; London subscriptions received by N. M. Rothschild
1824	Austrian Government 5% Loan, £3.1m, with Baring Brothers & Co., and Reid, Irving & Co.
1824	Alliance Marine Assurance Company £5m of shares
1824	Brazilian Government 5% Loan, £1.7m, with Thomas Wilson & Co.
1824	Neapolitan Government 5% Loan, £3.5m
1825	Brazilian Government 5% Loan, £2m, the remainder of the original £3m proposed to be raised by the Brazilian Government in 1824
1825	Government of the Grand Duchy of Hesse 4% Loan, 6m florins, by all the Rothschild houses
1829	British Government Treasury Bills, £3m
1829	Brazilian Government 5% Loan, £800,000, with Thomas Wilson & Co.
1830	French Government 4% Loan, f80m (c.3.2m)
1830	Prussian Government 4% Loan, £3.8m
1831	Dutch Government 21/2% Loan, £500,000

1832   Belgian Government 5% Loan, £3.7m with de Rothschild Frères

1833   Greek Government 5% Loan, £2.34m

1835   Portuguese Government 3% Loan, £4m

1835   Danish Government 5% Loan, £3m

1835   West India Loan, £15m

1838   Belgian Government 3% Loan, £2.75m

1839   United States Bank Loan, £900,000, with de Rothschild Frères

1839   British Exchequer Bills, £5.5m

1841   French Government 3% Loan, f150m (c.£6m), de Rothschild Frères, with N. M. Rothschild & Sons

1844   Belgian Government 21/2% Loan, £6.2m, de Rothschild Frères, with N. M. Rothschild &Sons

1845   Northern of France Railway, f150m (c.£6m)

1845   Lyons, Paris, Lille Valenciennes Railway, f200m (c.£8m)

1847   Irish 3% Loan, £8.9m, with Baring Brothers

1852   Austrian Government 5% Loan, £3.5m, of which £2.25m reserved for N. M. Rothschild & Sons, the rest reserved for subscription in Frankfurt

1852   Brazilian Government 41/2% Loan, £1.04m

1854   Eastern Railway of France, f62.5m (c.£2.5m)

1855   British Government 3% Loan, £16m

1855   French Government 41/2% or 31/2% Loan, f 750m (c.£30m)

1855   Turkish 5% Loan, £5m

1856   British Government 3% Loan, £8.9m

1856	Imperial Lombardo Venetian and Central Italian Railway Company, issue of £6m, concessions granted to the Rothschild houses
1856	Imperial Lombardo Venetian and Central Italian Railway Company, issue of £3.125m of 156, 250 3% obligations
1856	British Government 3% Loan, £5.4m
1858	Bahia and San Francisco Railway Company, issue of £1.8m
1858	Brazilian Government 41/2% Loan, £1.5m
1859	Austrian Government 5% Loan, £6m
1859	Brazilian Government 5% Loan, £503,000
1859	San Paulo Railway Company, issue of £2m, with P. Cazenove & Co.
1860	Brazilian Government 41/2% Loan, £1.37m
1862	Russian Government 5% Loan, £15m, with de Rothschild Frères, Paris
1863	Italian Government 5% Loan, f75m (c.£3m)
1863	Brazilian Government 41/2% Loan, £3.85m
1865	Brazilian Government 5% Loan, £6.9m
1865	San Paulo Railway Company, £200,000 7% debentures
1866	South Austrian, Lombardo, Venetian and Central Italian Railway Loan, £6m, with de Rothschild Frères, Paris, and M. A. Rothschild & Söhne, Frankfurt
1866	South Austrian, Lombardo, Venetian & Central Railway Loan, £3.6m
1868	New South Wales Government 5% Loan, £1m, with the New South Wales Bank
1870	Russian 5% Consolidated Railway Bonds, £12m, with

de Rothschild Frères

1870   Spanish Quicksilver Mortgage 5% Bonds, £2.3m, with de Rothschild Frères

1871   Brazilian Government 5% Loan, £3.4m

1871   Russian Government 5% Consolidated Bonds, £12m, with de Rothschild Frères

1871   French National 5% Loan, f2,000m (c.£97.5m stock), with Baring Brothers

1871   South Austrian, Lombardo, Venetian and Central Italy Railway Loan, £15m

1872   City of New York 6% Loan, $15m (c.£3.1m)

1872   Russian 5% Consolidated Bonds, £15m, with de Rothschild Frères

1872   Channel Tunnel Company Limited, £80,000

1872   French National Loan, f3,000m (c.£141.5m stock), with Baring Brothers and the Financial Agency of the French Government

1873   United States Government 5% Funded Loan, $300m, with Baring Brothers and others

1873   Russian Consolidated 5% Bonds, £15m, with and de Rothschild Frères

1873   Hungarian 6% Treasury Bonds, £7.5m

1874   Hungarian 6% Treasury Bonds, £7.5m

1875   Brazilian Government 5% Loan, £5.3m

1875   New Zealand Immigration and Public Works 41/2% Loan, £4m

1875   Russian Consolidated 41/2% Bonds, £15m, with de Rothschild Frères, authorised to negotiate the sale of £8m

1876	United States Government 41/2% Funded Loan, $300m (c.£62m), with J. S. Morgan & Co., and Seligman Brothers
1877	Hungarian 6% Rentes, £8m
1877	United States Government 4% Funded Loan, $700m (c.£143.9m), with J. S. Morgan & Co., Seligman Brothers and Morton, Rose & Co.
1878	Egyptian State Domain 5% Loan, £8.5m, with de Rothschild Frères
1881	Hungarian 4$ Gold Rentes, £16m
1881	The Bengal Central Railway Company Limited, £1m, with Baring Brothers & Co.
1882	The Rohilkund and Kumaon Railway Company Limited, £200,000,
1882	The Bengal and North Western Railway Company Limited, 4% Loan, £2.2m, with Baring Brothers & Co.
1883	Brazilian Government 41/2% Loan, £4.6m
1883	Hungarian 4% Gold Rentes, £5m, conversion by N. M. Rothschild & Sons and others
1884	Bahia and San Francisco Railway Company Limited, £298,000
1884	Hungarian 4% Gold Rentes, £10m, March, conversion by N. M. Rothschild & Sons and others
1884	Hungarian 4% Gold Rentes, £16m, September, conversion by N. M. Rothschild & Sons and others
1884	Egyptian Government, £1m unsecured
1885	Egyptian Guaranteed 3% Loan, £9.4m
1886	Bahia and San Francisco Railway Company Limited, £20,000,

1886   Brazilian Government 5% Loan, £6.4m

1886   Manchester Ship Canal Company, £7.25m, with the Bank of England at Manchester

1886   Chilean Government 41/2% Loan, £6m

1887   Chicago, Milwaukee and St Paul Railway 5% Bonds, $4m (c.£800,000)

1887   Russian Conversion

1887   Bengal and Nagpur Railway Company Limited, £3m

1887   Manchester Ship Canal Company 5% Preference Shares, £4m, with Baring Brothers

1887   Chilian Government 41/2% Loan, £1.1m

1888   Bank of Tarapaca and London Limited, £1.17m

1888   The Naval Construction and Armaments Company Limited, £225,000

1888   Brazilian Government 41/2% Loan, £6.3m

1888   Egyptian 41/2% Loan, £2.3m, with de Rothschild Frères, M. A. Rothschild & Söhne and S. Bleichröder

1889   Manchester Ship Canal Company 4% Mortgage Debentures, £1.3m, with Baring Brothers

1889   Burma Ruby Mines Limited, £300,000

1889   Russian Government 4% Loan, £27.7m, bonds issued to be applied to the conversion and repayment of railway loans of 1870, 1871, 1872, 1873, 1874

1889   Russian Government 4% Bonds, £49.1m, bonds issued as above

1889   Brazilian Government 4% Loan, £19.8m

1890   Russian Government 4% Bonds, £11.8m

1890   Egyptian Preference 31/2% Loan, £29.4m, with de Rothschild Frères, M. A. Rothschild & Söhne, S.

Bleichröder and Disconto Gesellschaft

1891   Manchester Ship Canal Company 4% First Mortagage Debentures, £453,000

1891   Ottoman Defence 4% Loan, £6.3m

1892   South African Republic 5% Government Bonds, £2.5m

1892   New Telephone Company Limited, £488,000

1892   Chilean Government 5% Loan, £1.8m

1893   Western of Minas Railroad 5% Bonds, £3.7m

1894   De Beers Consolidated Mines 5% First Mortgage Bonds, £3.5m

1894   Ottoman 31/2% Loan, £8.2

1894   Russian Government 31/2% Loan, £15.8m

1895   United States Government 4% Loan $62.3m (=£14.1m), issued with J. S. Morgan & Co

1895   Chilean Government 41/2% Loan, £2m

1895   Rio Tinto Company Limited 4% First Mortgage Bonds, £3.6m

1895   Brazilian Government 5% Loan, £7.4m

1896   Chilean Government 5% Loan, £4m

1896   Burma Railways Company Limited, £2.6m

1898-1901   Brazilian 5% Funding, £8.6m

1901   The Four Per Cent Industrial Dwellings Company Limited, £70,000

1902   Brazilian 4% Guaranteed Rescission Bonds, £14.6 m

1903   Chilean Government Treasury Bills, £1.5m

1903   Brazilian Government 5% Loan, £5.5m

1904   Transvaal Government 3% Guaranteed Loan, £5m, NMR tendered for £1.2m

1905   Chilean Government 5% Loan, £1.25m

1906   Companhia Lloyd Brasileiro 5% Sterling Bonds, £1.1m

1907   United States of Brazil Government 5%, £3m

1907   Japanese 5% Sterling Loan, £11.5m

1908   United States of Brazil Government 5% Loan, £4m

1908   Pennsylvania Railroad 4% Mortgage Bonds, £4m

1909   Chilean 5% Loan, £3m

1909   Grand Trunk Pacific Railroad 3% First Mortgage Sterling Bonds, £2m

1910   Brazilian 4% Loan, £10m

1910   Lloyd Brasileiro 4% Sterling Bonds, £1m

1910   Chilean 5% Loan, £2.6m

1911   Chilean 5% Loan (First Series), £4.9m

1911   Chilean 5% Loan (Second Series), £5m

1911   Chilean 41/2% Bonds - Copiapo Railway, £275,000

1911   Brazilian 4% Loan, £4.5m

1913   Brazilian 5% Loan, £11m

1913   Municipality of Concepcion 51/2% Loan, £100,000

1914   Brazilian 5% Funding Bonds, £14.5m

1914   Hungarian 41/2% Loan, £3m

1914   Austrian Government 41/2% Treasury Notes (with Schröders and others), £16.5m

1922   Chilean Government 7.5% Loan, £1,657,000

1922   Brazilian 7.5% Loan, £9m

1922	Czechoslovakian 8% Loan, £1,850,000
1922	Brazilian 7.5% Coffee Security Loan (with Barings and Schröders), £9m
1924	Japanese 6% Loan of £25m to facilitate reconstruction work in Tokyo after the 1923 earthquake
1924	Hungarian 7.5% Loan, £7,902,700
1924	Czechoslovakia Sterling Bond Issue, £1.85m
1926	Hungarian 7% Sterling Bond Loan (with Barings and Schröder), £1.25m
1926	City of Tokyo 5.5% Loan to aid reconstruction after 1923 earthquake (with others), £6m
1926	State of San Paulo, Brazil, Waterworks Loan (with Barings and Schröders), £2.5m
1927	Brazilian 6.5% Lan, £8,750,000
1927	Hungarian 6% Sterling Bonds Loan (with Barings and Schröders), £1m
1927	Consorzio di Credito per le Opere Pubbliche, Sterling Bond Issue (with Morgan Grenfell and Hambros), £1.6m
1927	State of Minas Geraes, Brazil Treasury Bills Issue (with others), £4m
1927	Brazilian 6.5% Loan, £7m
1928	Underground Electric Railways Co., London Debenture Issue, £4m
1928	State of Minas Geraes 6.5% 30 year external Loan, £1.75m
1928	Chilean 6% Loan, £2m
1928	Underground Electric Railways Co. Stock Issue (with Barings and Schröders), £4m

1928   State of San Paulo 6% 40 year external Loan (with Barings and Schröders), £3.5m

1928   Chilean 6% Loan, £2m

1929   Austrian Vorarberge Illwerke 6% 1st Mortgage Sterling Bond Issue, £2m

1929   London Electric Railway Co. Stock Issue (with Barings and Schröders), £5m

1929   Chilean 6% Loan, £2m

1930   London Electric Railways Co. Debenture Issue to pay for the extension and improvment of the Piccadilly Line and the provision of direct subway communication between Monument and Bank stations, £5m

1930   London Electric Railways Co. Debenture Issue for extensions and improvements to Piccadilly Line, £3.45m

1930   London Electric Railways Co. Debenture Issue for extensions and improvements to Piccadilly Line, £850,000

1930   London Electric Railways Co. and Central London Railways Co. Loan Issue (with Barings and Schröders)

1930   Chilean Treasury Bills Issue, £2m

1930   Japanese 5.5% Loan, £12.5m

1930   Austrian 7% Loan, £3m

1930   San Paulo 7% Coffee Realisation Loan (with Barings and Schröders), £8m

1930   Chilean Treasury Bills Issue, £2m

"At this point" I think that you cannot be surprised by the wealth of the family, don't you think?

Now, and only now, we are able to "understand" a small list of properties publicly attributed to them, only a few ... Maybe starting from the mother land of their empire: England.

Ascott House, Wing

Aston Clinton House, Aston Clinton

Champneys, Wigginton

Eythrope, Waddesdon

Exbury estate (in nearby Hampshire)

Gunnersbury Park (in nearby Middlesex)

Halton House, Halton

Mentmore Towers, Mentmore

Tring Park, Tring

Waddesdon Manor, Waddesdon

You can enjoy a visit on the internet if you are curious; anyway, look at the following residence: Waddesdon Manor.

Not to mention their love for french Castles from which many of their wines come from:

Château de Ferrières - Ferrières-en-Brie, Seine-Maritime

Château des Fontaines - Chantilly, Oise

Château Lafite - Pauillac, Gironde

Château de Laversine - Saint-Maximin, Oise

Château des Laurets - Puisseguin, Gironde

Château Malmaison - Moulis-en-Médoc, Gironde

Château de Montvillargenne - Gouvieux, Oise

Château Mouton Rothschild - Pauillac, Gironde

Château de la Muette - Paris, attualmente la sede di "Organisation for Economic Co-operation and Development"

Château Rothschild d'Armainvilliers - Gretz-Armainvilliers, Seine-et-Marne

Château Rothschild, Boulogne-Billancourt - Boulogne-Billancourt, Hauts-de-Seine

Haras de Meautry - Touques, Calvados

Château de Vallière - Mortefontaine, Oise

But what these things have to do with us?

Believe me, everything you have read so far is little more than "nothing" compared to what you can know.

We only need 'less TV, less Facebook, Twitter, videogames, fiction books and a bit more "proper research" and I guarantee that you will find a world literally incredible: non-credible!

But how can we take advantage of this news?

How can we use this?

Now we have perhaps become aware of being on the small, very small tip of a giant iceberg, but if by chance there were still doubts ...

Among the top 100 "economies" of the planet, measured according to their GDP, there are 49 states and 51 private companies, 47 of them American. So, apart 4 companies, all the others are American!

To understand the size of these companies, think to gather the sales volume of ExxonMobil, Walmart and General Motors: it is much more than the GDP of Saudi Arabia!!!

Now we can decipher some events and judging them in a less naïve way, saving our time from frivolous and common conversations leading to nowhere: news (you cannot do a thing), politics (your vote has 1/35 million value), economy (it is 80 years that the general price level and the public debt have been increasing) climate (tomorrow forecast... how will the weather be like?), sport (despite your favorite team wins or loses nothing changes in your life), economy (the book is entirely devoted to this subject).....

So, how can we use this knowledge?

For example we can be aware that no one nation will be excluded from the single currency, as for Euro or Amero for the following reasons:

We know the plan is to gather things rather than exclude.

Doing that, with the support of the people, requires an every changing tactic… it is really   a long-standing and demanding task.

The well-known debts of the states are towards the issuing companies that are part of the "great plan".

As we said, we are not speaking of money, that is no longer printed, but of electrical bits of the computer.

Now we can be critics with items such as money and banking system; for example, we can refuse credit lines or payments relating the turnover without an appropriate recovery plan. In other words, we should ask for a contract that includes the rights of both debtor and creditor, such as it happens when dealing with credit lines or mortgage loans, where the debtor can agree in advance an appropriate rescheduling plan in a given time and is not subject to a recovery plan at request, circumstance that destroys the entrepreneurship. In this way our bank will not transfer on us the effects of a possible crisis the central banks are going to originate after pumping enormous sums of money into the financial markets…

At this point we can interpret the politics of the countries in a complete different way, as we were watching at a football match or a tv show…

At this point we can opt out the naïve "hubble-bubble" that all the people does on what is told (the surface), "walk on new paths" and enjoy a well-off existence in our personal context.

At this point we can ascend to the heights and be part of the "big plan", why not?

Life gives us three options: join, move around or… fight!

From my point of view it is no worth fighting losing battles "ex ante" and, as the whole system is so damaged, I opt for the formers two options.

Ultimately, we are now aware and "respons-able": we are able to react to the "big plan", as long as we accept to play the game.

Remember our life cannot change just because we would like it or because we prey.

Life answers only to our actions. We use the word "Karma" with the meaning of "fate" or "destiny", but that word means actually "action". Our actions leave a mark on our destiny!

Now we have to discover the approachable opportunities and understand how to reach them with profit.

First steps

We can be "well-off" if we save money, not really "rich"!

Saving money means "economizing", it is only an operation of arithmetic: we cannot become wealthy only spending less than we earn.

To become rich we must focus on the dynamics of the entrepreneurship, the so-called variables, that is to say the "RISKS"

Economical risks as concerns the budget… Financial risks as concerns the banks…. Risks regarding the market demand… Political risks as concerns the new laws… Risks regarding competition among companies…

A lot of uncertainty!

This changeable scenario shows the reason why people like playing safe and have a safe salary, putting the chance to get rich into lottery or gambling.

Unfortunately, it is the worry of failure that makes a person unsuccessful.

The worry of failure freezes people and do not let them play the game, risk…

In the competitive world athletes are aware they can lose, but they do their best to win! Can you imagine athletes that run afraid of losing?

Do you remember the beginning of the book?

In sport you say: "if you think to lose you have already losen!"

So now we have to face the content of the previous chapter: " play the game"….

There are two different worlds where we can become rich: one is the entrepreneurial world, the other one is the financial world. Both of them are characterized by variables, that is to say risks.

In the following chapters I shall try to introduce you in a easy way – as my life itself shows – in the financial world…

Financial world *(for rookies)*

The "financial experts" always make me smile because finance is much similar to medicine, thus a non-scientific branch of knowledge, in contrast to mathematical sciences, such as economy.

A thing that life taught me a long time ago - and still now has been helping me – is to distinguish "dialectics" from "results". I did not acquire a high education diploma and, as I said before, at the age of 19 I was working as a waiter. This circumstance gave me a pragmatic approach to life: I think an individual shows respectability and authority for the results he reaches, not for his dialectics.

I learnt the finance branch lacks "reliability".

Not to skip on a banana skin, let us explore some aspects relating the "experts" of this branch:

Assuming it is not the amount of things an individual does but the results he achieves to characterize his authority, running out many financial transactions do not make you an influential person. I know people that run several transactions who got bogged down in debts.

The people really expert of finance, after a few years, are no longer salary earners that ask permission to go with their children to the dentist appointment *(?!)*

Moreover, once the financial career is on its way, the expert should no longer be interested in your money, but only in his own and in those of the banks, shouldn't he?!

And, if the banks gave him no longer money… well, there would be obviously a reason! Think that there are practically unlimited banks where you can borrow money. Does this mean anything to you?

This is why I smile when I meet the financial "experts", with all their mathematical certainty… and without credit from the banks!

So long I learnt we have to take precautions before giving people our money, but… as we know nothing about the financial world, we trust people that introduce themselves as "experts". All this happens because we go on refusing to learn the mechanics of that world! Mmm… don't you agree with me this is not the best choice we make?

For this reason about 4 years ago I started gradually learning the financial culture, with the commitment to stand "on my own feet" in the maximum period of 5 years.

As it always happens I knew that my mistakes would teach me more than the theory….

So I informed my wife we could lose money and she, in return, gave me back - one more time - an extraordinary support.

Going back with memory and thinking of all the years we have spent together, she never failed to support me even when I was feeling hesitant… she has always been a silent presence in my life, but really decisive!

Anyway, I was aware that through the mistakes we can reach the ability, or in other words,

"Practice is the only way that leads to ability, not theory".

I would like to point out it is the only way, not one way"

If you could metabolize this concept, you would make a quantum jump into a new life…. People usually stop exactly at this point.

Let us think: theory without practice does not teach you enough.

Books do not teach you how to cook, to paint, to be a good parent, a manager and either do not teach you a language... All the things we read refine the practice!

Instead, there several people that gain skillfulness trough a constant practice and ... no theory.

For this reason I think theory is a bypass to skillfulness, not the way to skillfulness!

How many well-known musicians ... unable to read a musical notation. How many excellent mothers... born orphans. How many athletes... that have never read a book. How many brilliant entrepreneurs... illiterate!

Why do only practice lead us to skillfulness?

A lot of things "in theory" are simple but when you put yourself to the test you find there is still a large gap between words and deeds!

So it happens you go wrong... well, <u>in your mistakes you find the message: the lesson</u>! So you try again paying attention to your mistakes... and if you go wrong again, you try again until the moment you will make no longer mistakes. In this way, mistake after mistake, you gain your skillfulness.

It is easy and naïve, isn't it?

Nevertheless people do not perceive the lesson that the mistake represents but the humiliation it carries, so they do not dare to go wrong.... And do not "do"!

For this reason I never attended courses on finance; I believe more in the exertion of studying, and it makes me smile since I have been an awful student!

Even if I teach, I am aware that two days cannot replace a book. Two days are fairly enough to perceive the subject, not to teach you!

A book can be consumed, used to debate or to confront....

I prefer to invite people to read books and my suggestion for a good start to understand, in an easy way, the subject of money and the magic world that turns around it, is "Business School" of Robert Kiyosaki.

Later on I realized that I had already learnt accidentally from experience the concepts he explains in his book. How lucky I was!

Anyway do not allow the case to manage your life: read the book.

An annotation, a little bit unusual:

I do not suggest you to read a lot but I suggest you to study a lot, expecially before you choose another book.

I use to read the same book even 12/15 times… I go on studying 5/6 books at a time until I metabolize them.

I take notes and write the most significative concepts on my notebooks rather than criticize what I read. Why not?

Now we are going to examine the three most important markets leading to the financial freedom, but before doing that let us distinguish the words "earnings" from "Income" and "Rich" from "Financial Culture".

Ricco e Cultura Finanziaria

Let us start with the difference between "Income" and "economic rent".

The income is the value of the goods and services produced by an activity; instead the economic rent is the income coming continuously from the mere possession of an economic good, it is automatic.

In other words, the income is represented by a revenue you have when you offer goods or services; instead the economic rent is represented by money that produces other money!

The word "rich" defines people that have a lot of money referring to their social context; note that each economy has its own level of wealth.

We know that in certain countries the money to buy an apartment in Milan make you "rich".

Not necessarily the people with a lot of money have a culture in the financial world.

In that world money makes money, the automatic revenue - the economic rent: lease, parking, patents etc - gives you money.

You can become rich without having a rent, as for well-known surgeons... dentists... lawyers... (I call it "risky wealth").

All the eminent people that reach the notoriety can earn consistent sums of money and even make a fortune, but, remember, always in return for their performance.

Think of a well-known dentist that, in an accident on a ski jet or skiing, fractures the wrist and the hand he uses for working...

At that very moment his revenues stop!

Do you understand why it is important to keep an eye on the possibility to have always automatic income?

Apprehending the financial culture, I also apprehended new perspectives such as:

Money is energy and <u>the economic upturn is always set by the input of money into the market and its flow.</u>

To make it clear, think of a man who buys a dress for his wife on the condition that, if it is too small, he can bring it back.

He gives a banknote of 500,00 Euros to the shopkeeper.

The shopkeeper uses the banknote to pay his debt to the petrol pump attendant who, the same day, uses the banknote to pay the mechanic who repaired his car.

The mechanic uses the banknote to buy his daughter a dress for the holy communion, in the same shop where the first man buyed the dress for his wife.

One hour later the man who wanted to make a gift to his wife goes to the shop and gives back the dress, that does not fit, and the shopkeeper gives him back his banknote of 500,00 Euros.

Shopkeeper > Petrol pump attendant > Mechanic and again shopkeeper... the same banknote allowed everybody to estinguish their debts, pay jobs, buy and finally come back to the first owner!

This is why at the moment the banks have the lead of the crisis and keep this situation stable until the moment they will change their politics and address it to the public sector instead of the government, as it is now.

Antonio Castro, in "il Giornale" 14/7/2012 writes:

"Of the 100 billion dished out by the ECB to give breath to the Italian economy, the banks purchased $ 92 billion of government bonds (they gave that money to the state and did not put it into the market). This gave 3% interests back while the ECB was asking 1% interests..."

Governor Draghi assured it would have been an inquiry but…

Nothing happened! Anyway, the banks involved in the business had a profit of 2 billions of Euros with no stress or risk.

Well, the conomy of our country?

This seems not to be their business.

Try to be astound, otherwise it seems you are not playing the game.

Even if…. Someone gets fun anyway!

You see, these facts do not taste new at this point, do they?

We are not living really a period of crisis or recession, but a period of social methamorphosis, thus economic methamorphosis, in which things are changing and never will be as before.

As in this circumstance the government is growing more and more greedy, we should think of proper tactics.

Basically, I believe there are still oasis to keep in consideration and pinpoint 4 schemes:

Projects/patents, real estate, finance, network marketing.

Let us analise them separately and understand their financial potential.

Ideas and patents

Today a project can make you earn a fortune. Think of people that created a computer application, a website or an iPhone app, staying at home

To be successful in this area two elements are required: Competence and Insightfulness.

Surely, the fact you stay at home and can develop your projects with time management and no remarkable investment is valuable.

Moreover, you have not fixed costs and you are subject to taxation only if you succeed and earn money. This is not an evaluation to omit, if you think of the direction economy is taking…

I am not going farther because nobody can give advice or transmit his experience on items such as competence and insightfulness

The point is to create something people consider useful or enjoy. Any kind of pleasure.

<u>No crisis enables people to look for pleasure</u>. People who smoke do not stop because of the crisis.

You see that despite the recession, stadiums are always crowded and people use to make trips during the holidays. The day the iPhone 5 was commercialised, it registered a burst of sales, although it is very expensive.

So, it is a sort of challenge about things that may be considered useful, amusing or pleasant.

Real Estate

Despite what is commonly said, the sector of real estate is still now offering good opportunities, though <u>the scheme used in the past does not work any longer</u>: you buy from a private and then you transfer your property to others...

As I got to share before, we are creating a "new" community and nothing will be like before ever again.

Unfortunately, nostalgic people hope for it and the more hopeful "wait"...

We are looking at a new era, which therefore needs a "new" approach.

Therefore, we must first discover what has changed in real estate.

Small golden rules:

As always it had been, and it is still now, you make business <u>not</u> when you sell the apartment, but when you buy it. If you bought the apartment at a lower price than its real value, you can sell it easily!

The estate agents do not let you make business... if the business exists, they will make it on their own with the money of the banks or the help of some friends.

You can make good business and buy at a price "extremely low", only in "extreme" situations as it happens when you buy from a judicial auction.

Do you remember the plungers?

We all are plungers when we are involved in asset stripping, even when talking of a shop: we profit of someone with financial straits, but, at the same time, if we do not his financial difficulty grows.

Given the premises, we can start. Please, note that to buy your own apartment does not belong to the financial culture but to the economic culture, that – for its intrinsic characteristics – will never make you rich.

The economical approach makes people think: " it is better to ask for a mortgage than to give money to the homeowner…" Yes, of course it is, but this reasoning concerns the economic field, absolutly not the financial one!

Do you remember?

"In the financial culture money must create other money" … So, if you have enough money you buy a house to speculate, to make more money, not to "protect" yourself.

In this way, you buy a house to sell it and make a profit … .and you rent a house to live in.

I will try to explain in an easy way a concept, contrary to the popular beliefs our parents and the society gave us.

Remember: crisis and opportunities live together with a changing ratio. We have to understand which opportunities can be disclosed by this crisis.

Even in this case, we are moving countertrend, if you think of the mediatic world that makes us featureless, resigned to the crisis only to fit a big plan that asks us to return quietly to the fold, after having been bleed.

Damn, don't you think these pages can introduce you to a "new" life?

Let us go back to "speculations" on real estate and to the reason why to buy your own house do not belong to financial culture.

Think before buying a house

Let's take a look at the new parameters of our society entangled into the bank "credit crunch".

(do you understand the meaning of this term from our point of view?)

The banks today have been granting fewer mortgages than some years ago and people cannot buy houses easily. For this fact, a lot of houses have not been sold and the value dropped by 30% - 40%.

This is a good opportunity, if we are thinking to buy a house.

Moreover, for the benefit of speculators, the banks have been prosecuting the borrowers that could not pay the mortgages and now have become owners of an incredible amount of houses.

A lot of these houses pass through the judicial auctions with a valuation of 30% less the ordinary value that is already low.

A really lucrative financial operation is buying a property <u>before it is put up to auction</u>

I am not going to edit a compendium about this technique, I'd rather address you to the specialistic literature, but I want to pinpoint that the goal is to anticipate the bank and do not allow it to dispossess the owner, so that you can make the business before the property is sold at auction.

Banks are not really eager to manage real estate because it takes a lot of time to sell it at auction and unforeseen events may happen.

On the other side, the owner does not want to result publicly indebted to the bank.

In any case this maneuver is going to reduce the cost by the 10% and allows you to buy with a total reduction of 40% the original value!

That's the business! Do you get it?

Small investment, big return (maybe bathrooms and kitchen have to be renovated, as ladies usually wish).

You can buy stocks of the previous years of tiles and toilets on the cheap and have a great impact; finally, you paint it white and the house can be placed again on the market.

I am going to explain putting it into figures the reason why I suggest you not to buy the house where you live... unless you have a whim to be satisfied.

First of all, the annual rent of an apartment is about 4% its value and it is far less the mortgage we pay if we buy an apartment. Thus, an apartment whose mortgage is 1.000,00 Euros has a total value that is lower than an apartment whose rent is 1.000,00 Euros.

To be clear: an apartment that you pay 1.000,00 Euros per month has about a value of 300.000,00; instead a mortgage you pay 1.000,00 per month is relating to an apartment of about 200.000,00 Euros of value.

Think that you own an apartment of 300.000,00 Euros that you are renting at 1.000,00 Euros per month.

People usually think that it is better to buy an apartment – even if it is a small one - than giving 1.000,00 Euros to the owner renting it.

It's not really wrong from an "economic" point of view, but it is from a "financial" point of view. Now we are going to understand why, but we need to think as if we were "investors" speculators.

You will get the property of the apartment at the end of the mortgage, after 30 years. All the money you invest in this operation will give results after 30 years.

This does not represent a financial dynamic: money has to circulate and money has to be invested!

Let's see how to create money.

Think to use 1.000,00 Euros per month for a rented apartment and the same amount of Euros per month to get a loan of 220.000,00 Euros.

As every operation needs notary deed and has taxes, we can reasonably think to focus on an apartment of about 200.000,00 Euros and pay 15.000,00/20.000,00 Euros for the additional charges.

Then, if we buy an apartment before it can be sold at the judicial auction, we can become owner with a cost lower than its actual value of 40%. In this way we can focus on an apartment of about 350.000,00 Euros.

Moreover the bank is keen to give mortgage to people who have bought an apartment at a cost of 40% less, because that apartment will be the guarantee of the mortgage.

Once renovated (let's say a cost of 30.000,00 Euros) we can put it into the market, at a cost of 300.000,00 Euros, 50.000,00 Euros less of its actual value. A good business for the buyer!

On the basis of an investment of 260.0000,00 Euros (220.000,00 + 30.000,00), we cash in 300.000,00 Euros ahd gain 50.000,00 Euros. We made this operation with money from the bank!

Let's subtract the cost for renting the apartment, 12.000,00 per year.

50.000,00 Euros − 12.000,00 Euros = 28.000,00 Euros and <u>here we are, ready for a new operation, then another one and another one for 30 years!</u>

<u>This is the so called financial culture!</u>

I hope to have been exhaustive and for more references look at "Business School" by Robert Kiyosaki (the book I suggested you before)

It is a demanding activity, because not all the apartments are "interesting". Then, you should take part at 20/30 auction before buyng an interesting property (the more the offers, the less the business).

As I already told you, I do not personally like things that require "my time", since I don't find it "financially" correct (remember? Money that makes money, not time for money). This is why I delegate my real estate actions to those who are more competent.

He is in charge of everything, from finding the right opportunity to its conclusion and then we split everything: taxes payed!

He has now become a dear friend of mine and this friendship gave us the opportunity to reverse our financial interests in other areas where I'm more expert than him…for now!

The real estate has a financial exposition that comes from mortgages, but also from a nearly guaranteed outcome, whose main variable is the time between buying and selling. The shorter it is, higher will be the profitability.

Regarding taxes, it has the same benefits as the one before: you pay the taxes on profits and, therefore, only when the transaction is concluded.

Financial Markets

Do not fear, I'll pass by in an easy way over this topic, but believe me that it's already simple on its own. There are many "uncontrolled variables". This explains why there are few wealthy experts in this area.

As long as it operates in this world you never know "how much" you're earning, neither losing, because you can earn big numbers, but with the same speed lose so many!

It is often seen people becoming wealthy and then losing all their money.

We speak about Shares (acquire shares of a company), Forex (currency exchange), Margin Setting/Options/Futures (buy equity shares) and more...

It is a big and large world, full of variables and pitfalls, where the dynamics are: information, emotion, and...a lot of philosophy.

First of all we need to be sure to overwhelm our emotions over money otherwise we are stuck with fear...and fear never suggest the right things to do.

It's a world in which what you have in return is proportional to the risk, therefore whoever does not want to risk (like the majority of people) does not take advantage.

Personally, I work in this area with a small amount of money, that I consider as my "cash", in other words "money which is immediately available". This is because if the bought shares is "losing" its value and becoming less profitable than when it has been bought, with a simple "click" that amount of money is back in its old state.

It is obvious that you may feel more secure if you have a broader "wallet" so that when you need to "withdraw" you will always have some options that have more value than the price you paid them.

Personally, between all the possibilities (Shares, Forex, Margin setting, options, futures), I now prefer to work in the "options" area, but only in long terms.

Options offer a "financial lever" that shares don't, but they have an expiration date.

This means that when the options expire you may have earned money or lost money. Nothing can then change.

The shareholder allows the owner to keep his package for how long he wishes, but if you are "fast" investors (hit and run) you are forced to fast and immediate trading and this can be stressful and time consuming, since you must be in front of a computer to do this.

It is possible to do business within weeks instead of having to wait for months or even years. The important thing is to keep updated and, therefore, keep an eye out for the market.

If you do not have a speculative approach, the stock market has always been advantageous in 5 years.

On this topic too there are loads of books you can read...

In my case, since I do not like things that require "my time", I have monthly intervals.

I do not understand being stressed out just to make money, and this I owe it the path I chose to take in the last 20 years and that allows me to live with economic rent.

This topic too has many books to read!

You can have a first view of what is available to you with a "free" meeting with the financial advisor of the bank, but...

You must have specific questions because "he" is afraid of risking and therefore he will offer something "secure".

As for taxes, the bank takes care of everything and the transactions are entered each year, therefore taxes are paid on capital gained.

The moral of each one of these areas is the same: it is our decision to learn and to become skilled.

"Whatever you do not control...is out of control" and this is never a good choice.

Network Marketing

Network Marketing is also known as *"Multi Level Marketing"* (MLM). Both mean the same thing.

People have many different ideas regarding Network Marketing by what they manage to hear talking with others o by intuition...but we cannot rely on neither of them, don't you think so?

Very "authoritative" people in the financial world, like Warren Buffet, Donald Trump, Robert Kiyosaki and many others, define the Network Marketing as the perfect model of pure finance in which, without any capital, you can start your own business.

Yet, despite this, I am fascinated by how people do not want to learn more in depth about Network Marketing, or worse, are convinced they know everything, without ever being devoted to explore the "financial" world!

In fact, a typical objection is: "But I can not sell."

Everyone seems to have "opinions", but to the specific question: "What have you personally read or seen?", 90% answered "I heard about it".

One of the biggest misconceptions, as well as a symptom of ignorance, lies in confusing the Network Marketing with the Pyramids or the Chain letters and that's only because it has the exact same structure ... pyramid. Just like any social pattern!

Just think of the company for which you are working for, or politics, religion, army, hospitals, any Club .. Each of these structures is a pyramid!

It would be enough to know that both pyramids and chain letters are prohibited by the 173 of 17.8.2005 law everywhere in Italy.

Network Marketing is instead a "worldwide" commercial reality that exists since 1934 and is officially represented by all governments from its association with the DSA (Direct Sales Association), which in Italy is called Avedisco.

To better understand the phenomenon, official data of Avedisco say that in 2011 the sector accounted for a turnover in Europe of up to 15 billion Euros and 895 million Euros in Italy.

That said ... Which and what is the opportunity of "financial" Network Marketing?

"Create a commercial network" (not a pyramid or chain) independent and infinite, through individual motivation.

It is this second element to create the pyramidal structure: the motivation to be able to include as many people as you want, and they can do the same thing ... over and over again!

I see it as an "evolved" way of franchising.

We live in an era where we are buried by franchises, just walk into any mall in the world and you'll see it for yourself.

The difference between franchises and Network Marketing is that, the last one, enables you to become a Mr. McDonald, or even Benetton, Stefanel, Calzedonia, Salmoiraghi, etc.

Think about it as if the above mentioned brands gave permission to each affiliate to expand as they wish, following their beliefs.

In the Network Marketing - like in franchising - a high percentage of the earnings goes to whoever is in charge of the company and, he who gets the income has just a small percentage for himself, but over many people it doubles!

People, instead, think that you need to find an idiot that works for you, but, to be truly honest, the idiot is he who says it.

Let's see the dynamics: If you get 5 people and teach them the business (not a math game, but a job) and do the same with other people ... And they do the same ... You find yourself with 5 + 25 + 125 = 155 "dealers" ... 150 dealers created by only 5 people that you have personally chosen!

Can you understand why recruiting someone is the start and not the end of the activity?

You become partners of the same project.

Once this process has began, you will have economic rent, since everybody will eventually want to climb the marketing plan.

This explains the "pyramid" structure that attracts financial experts and that confuses a lot of us.

Not surprisingly, the famous tycoon Paul Getty said, "I would rather earn 1% of 100 people that 100% on me."

This means that the faster you enlarge your network of people the quicker you can earn a high amount of money that usually exceeds your usual paycheck.

First of all, though, it is important to know and understand a firms work before judging. This can be easily done by participating to the presentations that the firm does.

Researches show that 90% of the firms close in the first 9 years, therefore it is best to be cautious about the newness.

It is true that a change can be more easily positioned in the market, but what happens next?! After years as member of the firm, it would be a total disaster if it had to close. This is why a firm of MLM is an important aspect to be considered

Another important aspect of the firm is to see how well it is established in a global view. The international aspect of a firm plays an important role in understanding the success of the firm in the country in which it is operating and between its consumers.

What I am telling you now can be found in any MLM agreement, it does not only come from my personal experience.

Another important thing to keep in mind is what product the firm is selling: it has to be popular between consumers and it must be something that has a high rate of purchase.

The products must be of great quality to establish a loyal relationship with the consumer, since the products are supported by customer satisfaction and not with advertising campaigns.

This can usually be determined by looking at the firms turnover. If the products are valiant, more people will be demanding them and the turnover will grow.

Inform yourselves on the turnovers!

Before making your choice, be sure to attend to various presentations. This will help you to have a more complete view of your choices.

Concerning me, 20 years ago I started working for a company that did business in 12 different countries with a turnover of 400 million dollars (as you can see the tactic of having a complete perspective of your opportunities was respected back in the time).

It has been a good bet: the firm still exists today, its 33 years old, its listed in NY stock exchange and it does business in 88 different countries.

The 400 million dollars have now become 6.4 billion dollars, with a substantial increase of 1 billion dollars in the past 2 years despite of the economical crisis.

This is the true fortune that Network Marketing can offer: entrepreneurship, for few euros, in which the only variable is the person himself and his will to put himself on the line.

Thanks to this decision I live by economic rent, whatever I'm doing, sleeping, working, on holiday or even if I die!

(In my personal case, having 4 children, it was important for me the heritage of the company that I would have built, something that no one else offered at that time.)

Pay attention to the opportunities that MLM offers, not just for you.

For example, this business model has allowed me to involve my friend, the one with whom I said, I do real estate transactions. Remember?

His wife first and then he himself began and in just two years have been able to create a respectable income that allows them to take off a lot of fancies, including, most recently, a couple of dream cars.

I smile at the memory of when I was a waiter ...

Today I am 56 years old, I speak 5 languages fluently, I live in a dream house, with an unimaginable lifestyle that it is not only given by money, but by the complete freedom to manage our time and therefore decide what to do every day.

Do not forget that money doesn't give you the keys to freedom, economic rent does. This explains why wealthy people go on holidays, on their yachts when they want only on holidays, as everybody else!

It is not rare to find people owning enormous yachts that use them 3/4 weeks per year.

Once that you have built an economic rent, you can use each single day as if it were sunday, but this happens only after you have built your own business structure.

Action!

Finally, I want to point out that an "extra-ordinary" life does not represent a dream, it is the consequence of "extra-ordinary" choices!

Just ask yourself: "what are you especially doing to live such an experience?"

What are you doing to become an "extra-ordinary" person?

Which books are you reading?

What do you talk about with your friends?

Which "extra-ordinary" people are you spending time with?

Take a challenge; do not give up to fate, destiny or lottery…

"Now" is the moment to fight…

"Now" is the moment for…EVERYTHING!

Do not lose time!

As long as life can be, it will result in any case too short.

Learn, evolve; give a sense to the remaining time, do not waste time.

I am not speaking about how old you are but how many years

you still have to live… nobody knows.

I know people that would be in a young person shoes, but they do not consider that the young person may not have the chance to get old!

So, be response-able (responsible) to live an extra-ordinary life!

Outside, in the world, there will always be crisis and opportunities and..

<u>It is on you to choose where to place yourself!</u>

Se foste interessati ad approfondire l'immobiliare o il network-marketing potete contattarmi dal sito www.ccbastos.com

www.ingramcontent.com/pod-product-compliance
Lightning Source LLC
Chambersburg PA
CBHW050915260726
48660CB00001B/220